# HEADSPACE

# HEADSPACE

## The Psychology of City Living

Dr Paul Keedwell

Brimming with creative inspiration, how-to projects and useful information to enrich your everyday life, Quarto Knows is a favourite destination for those pursing their interests and passions. Visit our site and dig deeper with our books into your area of interest: Quarto Creates, Quarto Cooks, Quarto Homes, Quarto Lives, Quarto Drives, Quarto Explores, Quarto Gifts, or Quarto Kids.

First published in Great Britain
2017 by Aurum Press an imprint of The Quarto Group
The Old Brewery
6 Blundell Street
London
N7 9BH

© Quarto Publishing PLC 2017
Copyright © Dr Paul Keedwell 2017

A catalogue record for this book is available from the British Library.

ISBN 978 1 78131 611 5
Ebook ISBN 978 1 78131 712 9

10 9 8 7 6 5 4 3 2 1
2021 2020 2019 2018 2017

Typeset in Calluna/Calluna Sans
Printed by CPI Group (UK) Ltd, Croydon, CR0 4YY

MIX
Paper from
responsible sources
FSC® C020471

# Contents

# The psychology of the city

> How did it all go so wrong? . . . We showed them how
> to do it.
>
> Ludwig Mies van der Rohe (modernist architect)

More and more of us are living in cities. They can be stimulating, creative, inspiring places. As Samuel Johnson said, '. . . when a man is tired of London, he is tired of life.' But cities are also stressful, and they can be alienating. Rates of anxiety and depression are higher in our inner cities than they are in the countryside.

Urban design has an important part to play in amplifying or minimising these threats to our well-being. How our homes, streets, neighbourhoods and public buildings look, and how they are arranged, matter. These are not just aesthetic preoccupations, they are important for our mental health. Good homes, neighbourhoods and public spaces improve our wellbeing by buffering against the stressful demands of a working day.

Most of the time we don't notice the effects of the environment on our mood because we are too preoccupied with the normal trials of life. But the built environment affects us nonetheless. As individuals and as city communities, we need to think more about how we can shape the world we live in.

I am a psychiatrist and a psychologist who has spent the last fifteen years renovating homes in London. When I studied the history of modern architecture, I developed the theory that trends in design had mirrored new evolutions in psychology: the understanding, via Freud and Jung, of unconscious drives (the home can be thought of like the womb, for example); the study of human conditioning (different environments trigger emotions from past experiences); social psychology (how buildings and neighbourhoods can be prosocial or alienating); cognitive psychology (how our attention and learning can be influenced by design); and evolutionary psychology (how natural selection has shaped our preferences for different aesthetics).

The scientific study of how buildings affect our feelings and behaviours is a niche subset of environmental psychology, best described as architectural psychology. There is a lot of information out there, but it is surprisingly absent from the syllabus of an average school of architecture, and there has been no attempt to synthesise it in a way that we can all understand.

Buildings, and the spaces between them, enrich or enervate our lives, affecting how we perceive, think and feel. It is up to us to make sure that they work for us. Developers often build life-sapping buildings, dictated by the interests of commerce. Government buildings are often dictated by cost-cutting. Architects and town planners like to think that they know people and therefore know what will make them happy, but they have made a lot of mistakes over the years, and they are still making them. Much design and planning is guided by a kind of empathic intuition rather than any scientific evidence. The esteemed architect might be more concerned to make an artistic statement than to design a space that people actually enjoy using. Architectural psychology is often just a secondary concern.

Rem Koolhaas, the world-famous Dutch architect, is known for his interest in the ever-changing, fragmentary nature of the urban metropolis, and in 'bigness' in architecture. He has been involved in the planning of some of the megacities of China.

During an interview it was put to him that the Chinese practice of designing off-the-peg, high-rise blocks in under two days might lead to a less hospitable living environment. He replied: 'I disagree. People can inhabit anything. And they can be miserable in anything, and ecstatic in anything. More and more I think architecture has nothing to do with it.'

If Koolhaus is right – if people are immune to their built environments – then all we need is one-size-fits-all architecture and cities of monolithic, computer-driven buildings. This book is my attempt to prove him wrong – especially when it comes to high-rise living.

People demonstrably prefer certain aspects of architecture over others. We prefer a room lit by two windows instead of one. We prefer to walk along a high street that has a human scale, rather than a road serving warehouses or megastores. We like to look out onto nature. We mostly prefer streets on the ground than in the sky.

Buildings can have short- and long-term effects on how we feel. Sometimes, a building is exciting when you first walk around it but causes stress over time. Some buildings encourage exploration and play. Some shut it down. Some encourage us to be sociable, others are alienating.

The one lesson from history is that we never learn from history. Some of the mistakes that architects and urban planners made in the 1950s and 1960s are being repeated today: bad high-rise blocks are being built just as others are being knocked down. Some masquerade as luxury apartments, but they have the same social problems, just with a different skin.

Architecture critics speaking on archived BBC documentaries from several decades ago raise concerns that are just as relevant today – the ruination of city communities by seemingly unaccountable authorities and developers.

In the 1969 documentary *Shaffer's London*, the esteemed playwright Peter Shaffer tears into the Shell Building on London's South Bank, which he regards as architectural 'murder': the demolition of 'spacious, humane, original, life-enhancing, perfectly proportioned, elegant, uniquely London buildings' of the Georgian and Victorian age, swept aside for a building which is 'lifeless, faceless, hopeless, joyless, mean-spirited . . . a featureless life-despising mass, whose only message is that life is a prison . . . The people who designed this thing are, if you can believe it, the heirs of Wren and Nash. To me they are criminals.' He blames not only the people who commissioned it, but the people who let it happen – you and me.

Even in the new millennium it seems that we have given up fighting, leaving the future of our built environments to faceless professionals.

James Stirling, the late architect – held in such esteem that the Royal Institute of British Architects (RIBA) named its prestigious architecture prize after him – bemoaned how once-magnificent nineteenth-century British cities like Liverpool and Glasgow had been destroyed by town planners, motivated by the most efficient way to house the people. He did not always blame the architects involved, but the 'toxic combination of the town planner, the local council and the idea of progress . . . the idea that you have to take down and remake'.

Modernism, he said, 'functionalised the human being' in a one-size-fits-all, mass-production architecture. Ornament, he argued, is something we need for the soul. We need a building that has a personality and a face, that is more than a container.

Shaffer's contempt for modernity does need qualification: he overlooked examples of good modern buildings that had enhanced the lives of city dwellers. Many architects have learned from previous mistakes.

It is probably fair to say, however, that most cities around the world have been scarred by the utilitarian concrete frames of the International Style. We are all familiar with them: the rectangular concrete or steel boxes, with clean lines and flush, uniform and square windows. These are the legacy of the early modernists like Le Corbusier. Modernism set out to banish complexity and ornament in the pursuit of purity of design.

These buildings are placeless. They could be in any city in any continent. It is an architecture that ignores local context and scale – a context that was once shaped by the forces of nature and human need. You would need to knock down about one-third of the buildings in Birmingham, for example, to remove this blight.

In her introduction to BBC4's series of programmes on post-war architecture, Janet Street-Porter argues that public housing should aim to achieve the same high standards as the works of leading architects like Richard Rogers, Norman Foster and Zaha Hadid to avoid repeating the mistakes of the 1950s and 1960s. 'Architecture can't just be about ego, or structure,' she says; 'it's about open space, healthy living and social interaction.'

However, good cities require decent resources. After the Second World War, many local government authorities were under pressure to provide mass housing at low cost. As Norman Foster put it: 'The architect is powerless in isolation. He exists in a real-life world and he needs the inspiration of the client. And if you look at the political idealism, in terms of mass housing in this country, then it tells its own story. It's been very much about political statistics. It's been very much about expediency, short-term thinking, and not much to do with taking a longer-term view related to any more civilised concepts of lifestyle.'

A major reason for the failures of post-war planners was simple and profound – the people were not consulted. They were housed in places that accorded with what local government officials believed to be suitable – *their* ideas and dreams, not those of the people who needed to be housed. Also, they thought that their work was done after construction was completed. There was no nurturing and no maintenance, so the communal spaces and façades became shabby and neglected. In turn, the people felt neglected. If government generates the impression that society cares little about you, you will care little for society. The overplanned but unloved housing estate, and the community within it, will disintegrate.

One of the most famous failures of high-rise social housing was the Pruitt-Igoe project in St Louis, USA, which consisted of thirty-three monolithic, thirteen-storey blocks of flats, providing 3,000 homes, but without any organisation of the spaces between them. There was no personal or communal ownership of these spaces, and crime took hold. Indeed, it became so endemic that all 3,000 flats were entirely demolished in 1972, just seventeen years after they were built (see below).

The demolition of Pruitt-Igoe, St Louis

The Maiden Lane development in north London was built in 1983 with a decent amount of funding. More than 1,000 people were housed there. Playgrounds, community halls, squash courts, shops, pedestrian routes and public squares were integrated into the plan. Within two years it had become shabby and neglected. The council did not put enough effort into its upkeep, but the main problem was that, unlike Pruitt-Igoe, it was *overplanned*. The architects had prescribed how people should live. Again, there was no consultation with the people residing there and no sense of ownership.

It need not be like this. Architecture can and should have the ordinary person at its centre. But how do we argue for something better if we are not armed with the evidence on how buildings affect our happiness? We need the data to show the psychological and social harms of bad housing and misguided town planning. We also need to make sure we learn from past mistakes by going back and studying buildings that have already been built. We must take a look, too, at good housing schemes, healing spaces and sociable, life-affirming public buildings.

Architectural psychology sets up a hypothesis about how a group of people tend to react to a particular place. There are observations that appear to be universal (like the need for access to nature). Within these generalisations, there are individual differences in psychological need, depending on age, gender and personality, and these require a deeper dip into the data. For example, women are less drawn to high-rise living and large expanses of glass than men. Men prefer more open landscapes than women, and favour open views over a feeling of refuge in a home. Extroverts prefer open-plan living. Introverts prefer more privacy.

Sources of evidence vary from anecdotal reports to more controlled investigations, comparing different individuals in the same environment or similar individuals placed in different environments, either in the lab or out in the real city.

The quality of the data arising from this research is variable, and it can raise more questions than it answers, but important truths emerge about how psychology should guide the design of homes, towns and cities. Like many conclusions about psychology, once they are known they are seen as just 'common sense'. That's fine, as long as our architects and planners start to see it that way.

The purely artistic and the purely functional designers will both fail us. The best designs bridge the gap between art and function. Science is concerned with the expansion of knowledge, while art is concerned with the expansion of experience. Architectural psychology bridges the gap.

Given that most of us are not in a position to design our homes from scratch, we can at least try to find one that matches our particular needs. If our choices are limited we can learn to adapt more effectively to what we've got – allowing for our unique personalities and our stage of life. We can try to nurture those aspects and develop them. Or we can compensate for the impoverished architecture of some dense city blocks by spending more time in other, healthier places.

This book is structured like a journey – from the inside of the home to the wider cityscape, with its public buildings, parks, schools, workplaces and hospitals. We will travel through the different domains of living, of ever-increasing scale, each with their own influence on our mental wellbeing. We can all become architectural psychologists, and in so doing, lead a more contented city life.

Part One

# The Home, From Inside Out

We spend 90 per cent of our time indoors, and most of that time is spent in the home. In 2009 I conducted a survey of 1,000 homeowners all over the UK to assess how attached they were to their homes, and why. About one-third were not emotionally invested in their homes, despite owning them. We know that if we don't own a home we tend to be less attached to it, so in the general population this figure might be higher. We want to love the places we call home, but it is not always possible to do so. Sometimes the places where we live just cause stress and annoyance. Often there is a mismatch between the space we inhabit and our deep psychological needs: the problem could be with housing type, design, space, character or location.

Why do our homes have such an important influence over our well-being? In psychological terms, what does a home represent? Freud said that the home is a womb: it is the place whence we all emerged and to which we like to return for safety, warmth and sustenance. Jung regarded the home as a cave. Both men imply that the first function of a home is to provide refuge and security. Security is the second step in Maslow's hierarchy of instinctive psychological needs (the first being basic sustenance). Abraham Maslow can be thought of as the first evolutionary psychologist, and his hierarchy represents a useful model for understanding what a home and its neighbourhood can do to help or hinder our happiness. So, above security, we should be able to connect with others, have a sense of identity and positive self-esteem, and pursue our dreams.

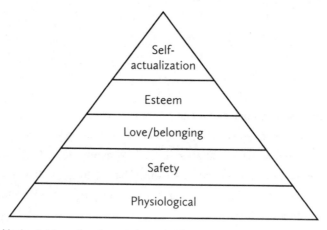

Maslow's hierarchy of needs (a pyramid)

Home should be the place where intimacy and sex happen, where we live with others and where we might, if we choose to, raise a family. Home should also allow us to express our unique selves – through the choices we make in decor, furnishings and memorabilia. It should reveal where we have travelled through life, literally and figuratively. In turn, our identities should be reinforced by where we live. Good homes can help us to express our true selves. Bad homes are so austere or overdesigned that they leave little room for homemaking, for adding biographical texture. The design of a home can help to inspire – just as is true of a vibrant neighbourhood and access to good public buildings – or it can inhibit our creativity.

Judith Sixsmith, of the University of Surrey, UK, used a method called the Multiple Sorting Task to obtain a detailed picture of how we conceptualise our homes. Participants provided descriptions of all past, present and possible ideal homes, along with places never considered as home. These descriptions were then sorted into categories. She confirmed that the main themes were to do with belonging, responsibility to family and self-expression. Home was where formative experiences happened (thus giving a place meaning) and where relationships developed. It was a place for entertaining friends. However, home also had associations with ideas of permanence, familiarity and constancy – things that are often lacking in people who rent in the city. For some, home was furthermore a place of architectural interest.

A home does not exist in isolation. Its location is important. What is the view from the window? Is the home twenty floors up in a high-rise block or on a street? What is the neighbourhood like? Does it have a sense of place, with a lively street life? Is the street open or closed to passing traffic? Does it have trees and green space? Are there hidden spaces where crime can proliferate? Is there a community and sense of ownership, or is it neglected? If a neighbourhood has declined, what are the causes and what can be done to reverse it?

What we learn from the psychology of the home extends beyond its four walls: so many of the themes we explore in the home run through the other chapters. For most of us, home cannot meet all of our psychological needs, and so we inhabit other 'homes-from-home' which can affect us in positive and negative ways. Let us first explore the idea of home as refuge in more detail.

# Chapter 1

# Refuge versus prospect

Home is where we are at our most vulnerable. It's where we eat, sleep, have sex, and recover from illness. It's where we start life as defenceless infants, perhaps have children of our own, and where we grow old and infirm. It's also the place where most of us would choose to die. If we don't feel secure in a home, it is hard for us to think of anything else: we don't sleep well, we become anxious, fatigued and even depressed. Home satisfies the primal drive to survive, to be protected from attack by enemies and predators when we are at our most unguarded.

The instinctive need for a cave-like refuge is apparent from an early age: as children, we love to build dens. Many of us remember making a tent from some blankets spread across chairs. Our den is supposed to protect us from intruders, but for obvious reasons it can't be a completely sealed box – the home must have a threshold to the outside world. We want to have a clear view out from our refuge for two main reasons, which have their roots in our early ancestral environment. Firstly, we have an instinctive desire to be able to see any threat approaching – any home can be invaded by a predator or enemy. It makes sense that the view is as wide as possible so that things can't creep up on you from hidden corners, forests or a thicket. Secondly, prospect helps us to look for sources of food and water, and enables us to assess the weather.

These two instinctive needs are in balance: too little refuge is (in our unconscious imagination) dangerous, but so is too little prospect. If your window on the world is too big, you will feel too exposed to predators – you will compromise the need for refuge. If your home is too enclosed, you will also feel under threat, and you will miss the strong desire to survey your territory. Too much of either will be stressful.

In the early twentieth century, the increasing use of reinforced concrete had the potential to open up the house to its surroundings more than ever before. Reinforced concrete floors could bridge wide gaps between reinforced columns, removing the need for support from internal or external walls. The external cladding of the building could be hung like a curtain (known as a 'curtain wall'). Windows that wrapped around corners became possible (with the columns set back from the corner edge). If you wanted to, you could enclose the entire building in a skin of glass. Some of the earliest modernist architects built homes like that. This was considered a good thing, because of the increased access to both daylight and natural views.

## Farnsworth House

A famous example is Mies van der Rohe's Farnsworth House, in Piano, Illinois, which was built in 1951 to much acclaim (see opposite). It is still considered a masterpiece of modernist design by many architects. A steel structure surrounded entirely by glass, it is known for its elegant, innovative design, but there is a secret history surrounding the building – a personal drama of conflict and misery.

Mies's Farnsworth House, Illinois

Its owner, Dr Edith Farnsworth, attempted to sue Mies van der Rohe, reportedly in the context of a bitter, unrequited love affair with the charismatic German-American architect. However, a re-examination of Dr Farnsworth's diary suggests that the emphasis on their relationship was a cover for a failure in the building itself. A less selective reading of her memoirs reveals that the lawsuit was less about romance and more about something more prosaic – that the house simply wasn't a very pleasant place to live in.

In chapter thirteen of her memoirs, Farnsworth recounts for the first time how she relates to her new home:

> By the end of 1950, it seemed possible to spend
> [the first] night in the house . . . It was an

uneasy night, partly from the novel exposure provided by the uncurtained glass walls.

Over time the house began to take its emotional toll:

> Do I feel implacable calm? . . . The truth is that in this house with its four walls of glass I feel like a prowling animal, always on the alert. I am always restless. Even in the evening. I feel like a sentinel, on guard day and night. I can rarely stretch out and relax . . .

> What else? I don't keep a garbage can under my sink. Do you know why? Because you can see the whole 'kitchen' from the road on the way in here and the can would spoil the appearance of the whole house. So I hide it in the closet farther down from the sink. Mies talks about his 'free space': but his space is very fixed. I can't even put a clothes hanger in my house without considering how it affects everything from the outside. Any arrangement of furniture becomes a major problem, because the house is transparent, like an X-ray.

Her modernist house, like the others, was sited in a desirable and safe rural location, but it caused a primal unease. None of us want to live in a state of total exposure, where any untoward visitor can see our every movement. Edith Farnsworth enjoyed no balance between project and refuge. The latter was sacrificed for the former. She wrote, 'The silent meadows outside, white with old and hardened snow, reflected the bleak bulb within, as if the glass house itself were an unshaded bulb of uncalculated watts lighting the winter plains.' Her anguished writings demonstrate that our desire to bring 'the outside in' has its limits.

While it is obvious that bedrooms need to be cave-like, the most pleasing and calming communal living spaces (where we spend most of our time) provide us with clear demarcations between prospect and refuge, signified in the theatrical balance between light and dark spaces. A great example of this is Can Lis, a house designed by the Danish architect Jøhn Utzon for his wife.

Utzon's Can Lis, demonstrating a clear demarcation between light and dark areas

In the UK, the long-running television programme *Grand Designs* has featured many big glass boxes over the years. Each episode follows individuals finding a plot of land and then designing and building their dream home, sometimes spending a huge amount of money. Entire walls of glass have become an enduring feature. According to the presenter Kevin McCloud, the dream often becomes a nightmare because most of the designs are just too big and bright. Interviewed by the journalist Sarah Lonsdale for the *Daily Telegraph*, he said, '... I don't enjoy living in a white box flooded with light. I like shadows, small spaces, old furniture.' Many owners, who had once talked of wanting to flood their homes with light, later regretted how large, open and complicated their homes had become. They had dreamed of bringing the outside in when, 'in reality,' says Kevin, '... they are looking out at misty northern hemisphere weather and have to think about getting curtains.'

## Gender differences

Experiments looking at the effects of different environments on our sense of security have revealed an interesting relation to gender. When males and females were asked to indicate their preferences for paintings of landscapes, females showed a greater affinity for landscapes with high 'refuge symbolism' than did males. Males did not reject refuge entirely but found it less compelling than the women. They preferred paintings with an emphasis on a wider view.

In another stage of the experiments, participants were asked to place a figure of a male or female adult in areas of the painting where they perceived the person would feel most content. Women tended to place both female and male figures in refuge settings, while males tended to place men in open spaces, and females in refuge spaces. The tendency for both genders to place women in areas of refuge might relate to reproductive activity – women who are pregnant or in childbirth are more vulnerable; but you could also argue that socialisation has programmed both sexes to regard women as somehow more vulnerable and in need of protection, while men are the protectors and hunters. There are many examples of primitive societies that show no such bias, and where women take on the hunting role.

What was less contentious was the third observation – that nearly all participants placed the elderly and young in areas of refuge, or close to them. So, although we all prefer an acceptable balance between prospect and refuge, it is important to realise that different members of society will set the balance slightly differently.


## Void to solid ratio

Let's return to the implications for the fabric of the home. As discussed, our threshold and view points have a powerful effect on how we feel: wall-to-ceiling windows make us feel insecure and anxious, windows that are too small cause us to be distressed by the lack of a view. So, is there an optimum window size? Research suggests that there is, but it will depend on the number of windows, the number of storeys in the building, and the size of its façade. What we are really asking is what is the optimal ratio of glass to the amount of solid wall in the building's façade? This is known as the 'void to solid ratio'.

In general, the ratio of void to solid varies with the function of the building. We are comfortable with high void to solid ratios in public buildings like offices and hospitals, but façades of places of worship, like Le Corbusier's Notre Dame de Haut in Ronchamp, in eastern France, tend to have low ones. Domestic ratios, which we are concerned with here, are somewhere in between. It was researchers based at Mu'tah University in Jordan who explored the optimal void to solid ratio for the home, in a systematic way.

The researchers used computer software to create sixty simulated building façades, of varying void to solid ratios and window orientations. The sixty images were divided into four categories based on the buildings' number of floors (one to four). There were five different window sizes, and three different window orientations. A total of 174 participants gave ratings preferences for the many building façade combinations.

The highest preference was for a façade with a moderate void to solid ratio of 43 per cent: just under half of a home's façade would be openings. This ratio felt transparent, light and open, but not too open. Provided the ratio was acceptable, participants also preferred the building with the largest windows, and windows that were taller than they were wide. Window heights of 2 metres were the most preferred, while those that were only 0.75 metre high were the least popular. These buildings felt far too opaque, heavy and enclosed.

Changing the number of storeys of a building changed preferences slightly, with slightly higher void to solid ratios being acceptable for higher buildings. However, there was nonetheless an inverse U trend in preference for an increasing ratio. As the void to solid ratio increased above the magic number of 43 per cent, preference began to decline. As we would have predicted from Dr Farnsworth's experience, having too much window is disliked.

Although the overall void to solid ratio had the biggest influence over preference, the size and proportions of individual windows was nonetheless important. Window height was more important than window width in determining preference. The caveat is that these preferences will have been influenced by the researcher's overall building design. However, they provide a rough guide. So, when choosing a building to live in, we think not just about the total amount of glass on its frontage, but also how this is apportioned across different window openings.

Preferences were influenced a little by gender: women liked slightly less enclosed buildings. In other words, they had a preference for slightly higher void to solid ratios than men. Preferences still declined as buildings became more open, just by a lesser rate than for males. This is surprising given the previous work on prospect versus refuge, where women regarded refuge as slightly more important than men. Perhaps it depends on your point of view. In this study participants were looking from the outside in. Previous studies were concerned with the inside out. There were no gender differences with regard to window size and orientation, or building size. Also, interestingly, variations in the imagined location of the building or weather conditions had no effect on preferences.

Overall, then, the results support the observation that very open homes like Farnsworth House are disliked. They also suggest that the horizontally aligned windows are not liked as much as tall, vertically aligned ones for example, the Embassy Building in Brighton. The findings are consistent with the fact that the most sought-after (and expensive) houses in London, New York and Washington are Victorian terraced houses with tall windows.

# Chapter 2

# Mystery and complexity

Why is it that when one man builds a wall, the next man immediately needs to know what's on the other side?

*A Game of Thrones*, George R.R. Martin

Research has consistently shown that we prefer landscapes which spark our curiosity. The most beautiful thing we can experience is the mysterious. An evolutionary psychologist would say that curiosity leads to innovation, which gives us an adaptive advantage. Curiosity and creativity are linked, and feed the greatest works of art and science. They are fundamental elements of human existence. 'He who can no longer pause to wonder', said Einstein, '... is as good as dead ...'

And so it is with our response to landscapes. A flat terrain fires nothing in our hearts. Where is the opportunity to explore a hidden potential for sustenance or shelter? Terrain that is partly obscured by mountains or trees is preferred over a flat plain. Research by the

American geographer Roger Ulrich also suggests that satisfaction is increased if some of the scene falls away, and is hidden. We like to anticipate a new landscape immediately beyond the limits of what we can see right now, waiting to be discovered, and this is likely to be underpinned by our instinct to explore.

The same is also true when it comes to the appearance of a home's interior. Narrow hallways entice us to explore and then reward us with a contrast – an open space, like a glade in a wood. They represent a trail of exploration through the foliage, which may hide treasures that other foragers have missed.

We like narrow passageways that lead you to larger spaces, both internally and externally

Late in his career, Frank Lloyd Wright designed a number of small houses that successfully satisfied our need for mystery and discovery. It turns out that we are most appreciative of homes which provide a wide space opening out from a confined one like the apparoach to the Piazza Plublico in Sienna (see above). Whenever we explore a tight corridor or tunnel, this is what we hope to find, and there is nothing more satisfying than having our anticipation confirmed by reality. Curiosity might kill the cat, but it is satisfaction that brings it back.

We tend to prefer less conventional layouts in the home: we are excited by their obscurity. Paul Pennartz, of the Department of Ecology of Habitat, Wageningen Agricultural University in Holland, conducted detailed interviews with residents of a variety of public housing projects in Holland in the 1980s. His aim: to determine what qualities of the internal design affected atmosphere. He discovered that when using several rooms in the house we prefer it if they vary in size and shape. Rooms that have corners are regarded as more functional than curved ones, but if the walls are not completely straight, this gives us more pleasure. Niches and nooks invite some novel use, and satisfy curiosity, as revealed by comments in the experiment such as: 'I like walls that aren't always straight up and down, so that you can build in cupboards and shelves and have built-in lights and things like that.' According to Pennartz a niche might not serve an obvious function, but it is not meaningless. The meaning comes from ideas about how it might be adapted to create something interesting to the owner.

Mystery is, however, a tricky customer. It can be overdone, and cause frustration. In Koolhaas's Casa da Música, a concert hall in Portugal, he creates a fragmentary maze of rooms around the central performance auditorium, with a significant lack of natural light. Quite deliberately, there are no consistent reference points to enable you to know where you are in the building at any one time. Visiting can be enjoyable in an explorative sort of way, but the experience soon becomes rather frustrating, depressing, even anxiety-inducing. The experience is distressing for the people who actually have to work in the building, day in day out. 'I hate this building,' a waitress told me, '. . . it freaks me out.'

The need for a clear exit is important, for instinctive and practical reasons. We dislike buildings that make it unclear where the exit is located relative to where we are in the building. Also, we do not like our entrances or exits to be too narrow and congested. Returning to the domestic scale, Pennartz found that the size of entrance halls was related to ease of communication and pleasantness. Thin corridors were not places for social interaction. As one resident put it, 'Crowding and pushing in front of that coat rack . . . when people are leaving or arriving at the same time . . . well, then you have to stand in a queue and if you have such a small entry where you have to stand one behind the other . . . that's not so pleasant, is it?' Square entrance lobbies were by far the preferred option over narrow passages. In summary, we like the interiors of homes to have a refuge, an element of mystery, within limits. We also like prospect – a good view of the outside – provided the total amount of transparency is not too great. For those of us lucky enough to be able to choose, what is the ideal landscape to look out on to?

## The perfect view from my window

It is obvious to most of us that we prefer to look out on nature. This is confirmed by the research of Ulrich and others, which demonstrates a preference for views of landscapes over cityscapes, and a preference for streets planted with trees and shrubs over those that are devoid of flora. The idea that nature is somehow restorative – a psychological tonic for mind and body – goes back to the Romantic poets, notably Wordsworth, and there is plenty of research to back this up. For example, modern life makes lots of demands on our attention, which leads to attention fatigue. Exposure to nature, even for a short period, can restore our ability to focus. This becomes very apparent during stressful life events like exams. A study by the environmental psychologist Carolyn Tennessen, of seventy-two undergraduates living in student dormitories, examined the effect of views of nature on their capacities to maintain attention, using a battery of tests. Views from dormitory windows were categorised into four groups ranging from all natural to all built. Natural views were associated with better performance on all measures of attention.

In London, many of the Victorian terraced houses are blessed with good-sized gardens, and these come at a premium. The Brits are keen gardeners, and even if they rarely venture into their gardens, they still like to look at them.

Londoners are increasingly re-orienting their houses and garden flats to reflect where they prefer to spend most their time. In Victorian tradition, residents received their guests in the reception room in the raised ground floor, facing the street. This was, of course, the biggest, most impressive room in the house, and for many decades afterwards Londoners tended to use it as their main living space. But things are changing. As the general awareness of design possibilities has increased, many homeowners have reconfigured their floor plans. Modest rear kitchens have been widened and extended to provide large lounge/dining areas with high and wide bifold doors right across the back of the house. The result: a panoramic view of nature, even if it is a managed, cultivated version of the living world.

Tenements in old European cities surround a planted and tranquil courtyard, as do the traditional *riads* of Marrakesh and Fez in Morroco. Again, the homes are arranged to maximise exposure to nature. As glass became more affordable, the upper middle classes of Victorian London frequently added orangeries to their homes, and conservatories populated by tropical plants. We cannot all afford such luxuries today, but indoor plants are a feature of most homes, as are pets. There is something calming and stress-relieving about being around living things, or representations of them.

## The need for nature

Why are we drawn to living things? Why do we have a psychological orientation to all that is alive and vital? The biologist E.O. Wilson has proposed that this 'biophilia' is innate because it holds the promise of sustenance. Our instinctive attraction to flowers, for example, may be due to the fact that they always emerge before fruits. They are an ancient promise of food to come.

We easily forget this, of course, because in modern industrial economies we rarely grow our own vegetables, forage for fungi or rear our own animals. Only those of us who live on farms or who keep allotments or vegetable gardens, even perhaps window boxes, are reminded of the real source of our food. The environmental psychologist Rachel Kaplan has studied the healing power of nearby gardens, and her work suggests that one of the most restorative elements of gardening is watching things grow. The promise of nature to provide for us is an ancestral memory etched in our DNA.

## Complexity and order

What we find so satisfying about natural landscapes is detail and variation. Roger Ulrich's work on landscape preferences determined that we like these factors to be inherent in natural views. We don't just want mystery, we want complexity. The same is true of buildings. In other words, our inherently curious minds are drawn to complexity. We prefer to see undulations, vegetation, trees, rivers and lakes, rather than a featureless plain. So, urban parks designed to contain trees and water features are visual approximates of a general class of natural landscapes that we prefer.

Similarly, it turns out that we are also automatically drawn to buildings that present us with complexity. At the micro level, Londoners prefer old London bricks to modern mass-produced bricks. The former were handmade from a mixture of clay soils, leading to a random aggregation of yellows and reds, while modern bricks tend to be more smooth and monochrome.


## Façade complexity

This leads us to consider the psychological effects of the complexity of a building's façade in general. Complexity is defined as the number of individual elements within a particular surface area, which have a noticeable difference from one another. The elements can be decorative and/or structural, like decorative brickwork, shutters, balconies, ironwork, roof projections, stonework, porticos, and so on. Research by Arthur Stamps at the Institute of Environmental Quality in San Francisco suggests that the silhouette shape and overall structure of the building's main surfaces is less important than the amount of decoration on the surface and the detail in the 'trim' around windows and doors. In fact, trim was the most important determinant of preference.

The Hong Kong Papers in Design and Development listed four main elements of complexity. Firstly, perceived complexity is increased by the sheer number of distinguishable features. Secondly, novel elements – individual styles not seen commonly, like in the façade of Gaudì's Casa Batlló in Barcelona – increase complexity. If we need to dissect what novelty means in architecture, it is about originality, dissimilarity, surprise and unpredictability. A third influence over complexity is the degree to which architectural details can be grouped together in meaningful ways. If these groupings become predictable, and form larger groups, complexity decreases.

The Birmingham library

Gaudì's Casa Batlló, Barcelona

Take, for example, the controversial library building in Birmingham. The architect attempted to add visual interest to the monolithic structure by adding recurring geometric shapes, like wallpaper – but the predictability of the pattern makes the façade less interesting. Compare this building with Gaudì's Casa Batlló, with its the varied proportions and textures (see above).

A final influence over complexity concerns the variation in appearance when seen from different perspectives. This is one of the reasons why Frank Lloyd Wright's Fallingwater is so revered.

Frank Lloyd Wright's Fallingwater home, Pennsylvania

Although a monument rather than a building, the memorial at Redipuglia in Italy exemplifies this idea. We can see how the steps leading up to the calvary have some complexity because of how they appear from different viewpoints.

As much as we like complexity, personal satisfaction requires some rational grouping, a sense of closure, as we shall revisit below. If there is no sense of order, then we tend to be overwhelmed. Even Gaudì's organic, sensual works have some rationality in the arrangement of their complex features.

The idea that we can become overwhelmed by too much complexity in a building's façade was explored by Aysu Akalin and colleagues at Gazi Univeristy in Turkey. Students were asked to rate a total of fifteen photographs from five different housing sites. These were allocated to groups of low, moderate or high complexity, based on the number of individual features. The researchers noticed that as complexity increased, so did excitement and interest. However, when it came to preference, it was the houses with a moderate level of complexity that were preferred the most. In other words, there was an inverted U relationship between complexity on the x axis and preference on the y axis. Too little complexity led to what the post-modern architect Robert Venturi referred to as 'less is bore'. We prefer to have to put in a certain amount of effort in order to understand the façade of a building – it is the need for mystery on a detailed scale. On the other hand, too much complexity was disliked. This is an echo of the effect of different natural landscapes on our psyche. We have seen that we prefer landscapes with some visual interest (trees, mountains and water), but which are not so crazy and wild as to be unsettling.

With more complex façades, as with wild, overgrown landscapes, we seem to reach our limit of information at the point where we can't assimilate any more. Once we feel overwhelmed we stop enjoying the view. We start to experience a state of conceptual confusion – a point where we can't make any sense of what we are seeing. To prevent overload, we need to be able to accommodate the unfamiliar elements with those that are more familiar. Of course, some buildings can be perceived as less complex over time, as we become more familiar with the different elements – a process known as appropriation. According to Akalin, this includes 'taking control over, becoming familiar with, investing with meaning, cultivating and caring for, and displaying identity and belonging with a place or object'. It's a process that evolves gradually, changing the meaning of the building.

The materials used on the outside of a building can bring about a variety of emotions and there are often gender differences in preference. Wood shingles and weathered wood are regarded as warmer and more feminine than brick, stone and concrete. On a larger scale, buildings that are most satisfying balance complexity with elegance. In my opinion, the Scottish Parliament building in Edinburgh manages to fail on both counts. It was designed by the Spanish architect Enric Miralles, and cost £414 million to build – and it is not popular.

The Scottish Parliament building

In 2008 the video-game company EA Games was launching its city-building game SimCity. As part of the marketing campaign it conducted a poll to determine which building the British would most like to see razed to the ground. The Scottish Parliament was high up the list, at fourth. The fact that it won RIBA's prestigious Stirling Prize for excellence in architecture illustrates the continuing gulf between some architects and the people they design for.

The front façade has some complexity: it is broken up by windows of varying shapes, with irregular bits of wood stuck across them in random arrangements. The rear façade, which looks out over public space, is almost completely featureless. The bigger structure, made up of blocks of varying size and shape, is designed to be fragmentary, like a Frank Gehry building. However, it lacks the cohesive elements used by Gehry (in the best of his buildings) to tie everything together – such as the use of consistent materials. Not only is its lack of elegance displeasing, its disjointed appearance actively makes you feel uneasy. It is hard to see how and why it fits together, and there is no particular joy in trying to work it out. Finally, the use of drab materials in a city which gets more than its fair share of grey days does not help. A few additions to the windows look stuck on, like an afterthought, and are not enough to compensate. When an architect tries to add complexity without any coherence, the building can engender an uncomfortable sense of disorientation and lack of closure – a concept we will now explore a bit more.

Chapter 3

# Closure

The human brain is always looking for order in apparent chaos. This fact has spawned a whole field of psychology and therapeutics, collectively known as Gestalt psychology. It explores how what we view is usually changing all the time – in terms of field of view, angle of view, different lighting conditions. We need a mechanism for finding constancy and continuity in this ever-changing sensorium. If we could not, we would be in a constant state of disorientation and confusion.

Sometimes we like to feel disoriented – it gives us a thrill. We have an instinctive desire to explore new and complex environments. However, this is in an attempt to master them. If we cannot find some order or meaning in it, we quickly want to withdraw. We start to panic. It's a survival mechanism. If we cannot work out how to interact with an environment, it is not going to be helpful to use, and it could be dangerous.

We will instinctively try to make sense of complex patterns by using five main processes:

1. Figure-ground – In any scenes, we instinctively try to distinguish which objects are near and which are further away. The lack of any distinction between figure and background is unsettling.
2. Proximity – When certain objects in a scene are closer together, we will tend to clump them in groups, until we understand the bigger picture.
3. Continuity – We look for patterns within apparent chaos, and perhaps perceive objects as forming a continuum within that pattern, even when, in reality, they are independent.
4. Closure – We tend to see a finished whole (a gestalt) in an unfinished figure (we fill in the gaps).
5. Similarity – We group similar objects together (we categorise).

These are all ways of ordering and editing large amounts of visual information. They help us to understand what we see in as little time as possible. The instinctive drive is to reduce any anxiety that arises from disorder and confusion.

We depend on experience in this process – memories of previous similar objects that we have encountered and which form a conceptual category (like dogs or rivers or houses). We recognise the overall pattern, rather than being thrown off track by the detail.

We can see this process in action with two simple tests. Taking a look at the following images a triangle will be perceived in picture A, although no triangle has actually been drawn. B is a black worm wrapped around a white pole; C shows a sphere covered in spikes, much like a mace; D is a snake or sea monster swimming through water, buried beneath the surface at two points.

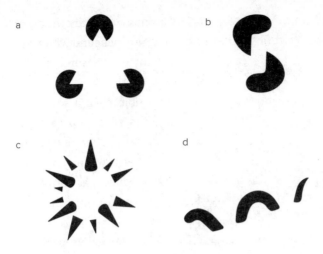

Examples of how we fill in the gaps to make a whole (a gestalt)

In all these examples we recognise disparate shapes as belonging to a single shape, where in actuality no such thing is drawn. We *fill in the blanks* to flesh out a complete idea. Pattern recognition allows us to grant shape and form to the nameless things we see around us.

Our minds can't avoid seeing the environment in this way, unless we make a supreme conscious effort. The image overleaf usually has no meaning for us. It is an unsettling mess of dots. It is unsettling because we are unable to find a pattern in it that makes sense, in terms of the categories of objects we have stored in our brains. We are unable to form a cohesive pattern, or gestalt. If we look at it for too long, we get information overload.

However, if we observe the flipped image, and then consider its title, *Dog Picture*, we perceive a dog. The gestalt emerges from the myriad dots. This happens almost instantaneously. We do not need to build it up slowly from all its component parts (tail, ear, collar), which would be exhausting. Instead a familiar pattern emerges of a dalmatian from the same picture transposed.

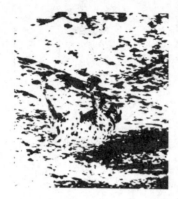

This idea can be followed through to architecture. We can have complexity in a building, but we need to be able to understand it as a whole. Without this understanding we feel uneasy. It is ironic that Rem Koolhaas, the architect of the deliberately confusing Casa da Música, said that 'without rules there is no play'.

Some scenes make us feel uneasy because we cannot form a gestalt from their myriad features. Landscapes and buildings need to conform with our understanding of the world. Nature and chaotic buildings can be too wild for comfort.

Ulrich's experiments proved that natural scenes are actively disliked if they are featureless (of low complexity), but they are also disliked if they are lacking in a focal point (like a forest setting cluttered with brambles and downed wood). So, a building without a focus – a clear entry point, for example – will also be unpleasant. This is about the perception of figure-ground, and interacts with the desire to have a good line of sight. In a landscape it might refer to the horizon. In a building it might refer to a clear view through the interior, so that we understand the limits of the building. We don't like shallow, disordered views, whether in the home or in the landscape. On the other hand, we do not want to live in a bland box – the built equivalent of a featureless desert.

There is another lesson to be learnt from Ulrich's research on landscapes (see Box 1). He observed that we prefer the ground to be smooth, not jagged and uneven. In other words, it should appear easily navigable by a human on foot. So, scenes that are savannah-like are particular favourites. We can think about how this translates to a building with an uneven floor, and how unsettling this feels.

---

**Box 1: What we like and dislike in our views of nature**

Likes:
1. Complexity
2. Ground moving away from view (the promise of more land to explore?)
3. A focal point
4. Depth – ideally a view of the horizon.
5. A water feature (river, lake, etc.)
6. Smooth terrain

Dislikes:
1. Disorder/chaos
2. Flat, featureless landscapes
3. No line of sight to a distant focal point – e.g. a dense forest edge with brambles and fallen trees
4. Rough and jagged ground

5. Specific dangers: sheer drops, predators, poisonous creatures (particularly snakes and spiders)

## Opportunity versus danger – the balance for survival

How can we explain these preferences? Are they all instinctive or are some learned? It is very tempting to return to evolutionary explanations. We have spent most of our evolutionary history as hunter-gatherers – we emerged from the savannahs of Africa. Complexity, in terms of trees and contours might give us more options for foraging, for play and for shelter: a mostly even ground underfoot would help us to forage, hunt and flee from danger. But, if we cannot immediately understand our environment, we can't do a quick risk assessment, to make sure we are safe from predators – can we see them approaching, and can we easily escape? A dense thicket, with no views through it, could hold nasty surprises. A predator could be close at hand, and we might be cornered. On the other hand, we don't want a completely flat and open landscape where there is nowhere to hide. Our liking of water presumably reflects our primeval need for hydration.

Another major influence on our preferences to emerge from Ulrich's landscape research provides further support for the evolutionary theory: the presence of specific dangers. So, the edge of a steep cliff or a dangerous animal has an overriding influence on likeability, irrespective of levels of variables such as depth and interest. The findings strongly imply that our survival instincts rule our aesthetic preferences.

'Preference', though, is a rather superficial measure. It says nothing about how different vistas affect our feelings.

The Faculty of Psychology at the University of Santiago de Compostela asked individuals to rate twelve landscape photographs taken in northwest Spain, giving not just a beauty rating but also an emotional reaction (gloomy versus happy, and boring versus stimulating). Perhaps not surprisingly, beauty was strongly associated with happy and stimulating judgments. Negative emotions such as stress and sadness were perceived as reduced by a number of important landscape features, including vegetation, hillsides, mountains, valleys and rivers.

A definite limitation of these studies is their potential cultural bias. In general, the participants have been American and European. Unless you can demonstrate that an emotional reaction is universal across cultures, it is harder to argue that it is instinctive.

A lot of what we perceive to be pleasant in the West might be shaped not so much by the survival instinct, but by the legacy of eighteenth- and nineteenth-century concepts of what is picturesque. To offer just one example, the landscape designer Capability Brown created gardens for the stately homes of England which captured the classically appealing composition of the Old Masters. In other words, old pictures, influenced very much by classicism, may have shaped our preferences in the real environment.

Does a nomadic African or Mongolian tribe have the same preferences? They do not have a picturesque tradition. Their preferences will depend on how they have adapted to their wilder habitats. Mongolian tribes use horses to cover large areas of open ground, so they might be less fazed by such exposed places than the members of a tribe in the East African Rift Valley. Would the farmer on the Argentinian pampas have the same dislike of wide featureless landscapes as a Londoner with a vista of Hyde Park? One study has attempted to examine the question of cultural bias. When comparing the landscape preferences of Americans and Australians of varying backgrounds (including aboriginals), it was found that their preferences were universally the same across all categories: vegetation, open-smooth, open-coarse, rivers, agrarian, and structures.

It is probably true that there are some universal preferences in all of us, shaped by our instinctive needs to survive and prosper, but other preferences are more sensitive to culture and context. Until more research is done, we might need to consider how the buildings we inhabit speak to both universal needs and local context.

We have considered the ideal view from our window – the perfectly balanced landscape. Realistically, many city homes will lack a garden or other view of nature, but this does not mean that we cannot actively seek it within our cities. Researchers have explored if we can adequately compensate for this by visiting a place of verdant recreation, or somewhere on the coast.

The society Natural England conducted a survey of engagement with nature in 4,255 individuals. Among other things, they investigated feelings of restoration (calm, relaxed, revitalised and refreshed) recalled by individuals after visits to different natural environments within the last week. Coastal visits and two specific types of green spaces (woodlands/forests and hills/moorland/mountains) were associated with the most restoration, and town and urban parks with the least. The longer the visit, the more the restorative effect.

Another survey, based in Finland, asked residents of its two biggest cities to describe their favourite places to visit. After two months the survey was repeated to see if their preferences had changed. Managed natural settings (mainly urban woodlands) and waterside environments were reselected most often.

Chapter 4

# Nature in the home

An alternative to visiting nature is to simulate it. Research suggests that we can benefit from including a sense of nature within the home – by including a landscape painting or photo, for example. The same rules apply to a photo/painting as in a real scene: an open landscape (such as a savannah) is more restorative than a closed landscape (such as a forest). It is a common rule of thumb among photographers that landscapes should be represented according to the 'rule of thirds'. A landscape is thought to be more appealing when the horizon is positioned one-third of the way up the photo (perhaps when the sky is more interesting), or two-thirds of the way from the bottom (when the foreground has some special appeal). Researchers at the Czech University of Life Sciences showed that natural objects of interest like trees, mountain features, lakes and so on triggered a more positive emotional reaction if placed on one of the lines of thirds, as opposed to halfway up a picture.

Anette Kjellgren, of Karlstad University, Sweden, was interested in how much the restorative effects of nature could be recreated in a lab. In the natural environment condition, participants were seated on a bench with a view of ancient woodland within the Karlstad Nature Park, which included 400-year-old pines, lakes and rivers. In the simulated conditions, participants sat in a windowless laboratory and were shown a slideshow of different views of the same park.

She examined how much each condition could generate increased energy and vitality and an altered state of consciousness, characterised by feeling more than thinking, thinking in the here and now, intensified sensory perception, a feeling of harmony and union with nature, increased sense of wellbeing, and a feeling of tranquility. Although the photographic simulation failed to stimulate the same level of altered consciousness and vitality as the first-hand experience, they were nevertheless increased in both conditions. Even more interestingly, stress was reduced by roughly the same degree in both natural and simulated environments. So, although real natural environments are more powerful in increasing positive feelings, a simulation of nature still has a powerful effect, especially with regard to making you feel calmer. Not only is it better than nothing, it will actively help to reduce stress and improve your well-being.

### Nature's colours – the green effect

Another way of simulating nature in the home is through the colouring of our walls. It has been suggested that colours derive their meaning from the natural environment. Dark blue is associated with passivity, perhaps because primitive man prepared for rest at dusk. Yellows and reds are active, stimulating colours, perhaps because they are found in the rising sun, heralding the beginning of daily activities. Grey-green walls are generally calming, representing the sheltering effects of a verdant landscape. So, bright reds and yellows make bad colour choices for bedrooms, but might be welcome as accent colours in kitchens, to stimulate us at breakfast, or in playrooms. Natural greens, ruddy browns and blues are suited to more relaxing spaces. So, careful attention to decor might help to compensate for the lack of contact with nature. Overall, adding colour to a home might lead to greater contentment over time than white walls, irrespective of the current trend for neutrality.

Being exposed to a flash of green colour might make us more creative. Stephanie Lichtenfeld and colleagues at the University of Munich conducted a series of Internet-based experiments to investigate this 'green effect'.

Creativity is consensually defined as the generation of ideas or products that are both novel and of value. In the first experiment, a white or a green rectangle flashed up on the screen just before participants completed the Unusual Uses Task, where they were asked to dream up as many different ways to use a tin can as possible. They were told that their ideas could be neither typical (such as using it to hold a soft drink) nor impossible. Amazingly, although only exposed to the green rectangle for a number of seconds, the participants who had viewed it were more novel, lateral and ingenious in their responses.

In a second experiment the researchers changed the control colour from white to grey, just in case there was an effect of brightness. They also used a classroom setting with a binder, instead of a computer screen, where the coloured rectangle was on the cover of the binder. They also used a different test of creativity – drawing as many different objects as possible from a geometric figure during the allotted time period. Once again, the green group did significantly better on the test.

In a third experiment, the colour red was included as a comparison, to be sure that the effect was not just about colour per se (compared to the achromatic grey). Once again, the green image provoked increased creative behaviours, while the red image did not. In fact, the red image did not stimulate any more creativity than the grey image. The researchers repeated the same experiment using the colour blue, wary of the negative cultural associations of red (spelling danger, or a need to halt). They found exactly the same result – only green differed from grey in its creative effect.

This is a fascinating and important finding. It is also intriguing. Why should this colour be linked to creativity? Several alternative explanations are worth considering: green is associated with growth, not only physical growth but also psychological development and mastery. Feelings of mastery have been shown to foster innovation and creative performance in prior research. Green is also a signal to go at traffic lights, races or in experiments. In many cultures, therefore, it is somewhat liberating in its associations, giving licence to creativity. An alternative explanation, building on Rachel Kaplan's work on the restorative effect of nature, is that the colour green, by virtue of its association with nature, encourages creativity by improving vitality and concentration.

Whatever the explanation, this series of experiments should encourage us all to think about how we might introduce green colour into our homes: perhaps by introducing indoor plants and window boxes, adding a landscape painting or a green-coloured wall. We might want to consider a home with a view of a tree.

## Nature's dimensions

Another way in which a home might ape nature is through its proportions. The 'golden ratio' is found throughout nature, including the spiral arrangements of leaves and seashells, and since the time of the ancient Greeks we have measured the attractiveness of a building by its conformity to this ratio (written as $1: 1 + \sqrt{5})/2$, or $1:1.61803398875 \ldots$). The longer dimension should be just over half as long again as the shorter one – or, in percentage terms, the shorter dimension should represent 62 per cent of the longer dimension.

The twentieth-century architect Le Corbusier used the golden ratio in the design of many of his residential projects – especially in the form of the golden rectangle, in which the ratio of the longer side to the shorter side is the golden ratio ($1:1.61$). He called his system the Modulor. Not only did he regard the Modulor building as more aesthetically pleasing from the outside, he believed that the ratio was more ergonomic on the inside. Hence, room size, ceiling heights and other internal features, including the placement of desks and beds, conformed to the ratio.

Le Corbusier was likely aware of the assumption that some of the most admired classical buildings conformed to the golden ratio, the most famous of these being the Parthenon in Athens. He was also influenced by Leonardo da Vinci's Vitruvian man, drawn at a time when it became fashionable to celebrate the hand of God's work in both man and nature. During the Renaissance, these proportions were imbued with inherent beauty and a deep spiritual significance.

The importance of the golden ratio in both art and nature has since been challenged. The dimensions of the Parthenon, when carefully measured, do not conform to the golden ratio precisely. And while the German psychologist Adolf Zeising found the golden ratio in the arrangement of branches along the stems of plants and of veins in leaves, his findings for animal skeletons and the branching of nerves and veins have been questioned.

When trying to come up with a Universal Law of Nature (or any law, in fact) there is a danger of confirmation bias – paying attention only to the data, in this case 'natural dimensions', that supports your theory. The best scientists strive to find evidence to disprove a theory before confirming that it is a law.

Professor Devlin of Stanford University has been conducting a study of student preferences for rectangles of varying shapes. Although the work remains unpublished, he has staked his reputation on the results he has seen so far. He has concluded that the students' preferences for rectangles are seemingly random. They do not, on average, prefer the rectangle that conforms to the golden ratio. Furthermore, there is no consistent pattern in their preferences: if you ask them to repeat the exercise, they pick different rectangles. Devlin concludes that human preference is complex, and that the golden ratio is not, in fact, more aesthetically pleasing to people.

Although Devlin might be right, the simple rectangle may not represent a sufficient test because it lacks complexity and meaning. It is not a building or a landscape. If a line drawing of a rectangle lacks salience, then why should we really care about judging it? If we don't feel engaged with the image, then why would our preferences be anything but random?

A much more salient subject is the human face. In Germany, a Dr Marquardt created the Marquardt Beauty Mask from the averaged dimensions of thousands of human faces. He then used computer morphing to alter these dimensions. He found that where the shape of the face (the width versus the length), as well as some of the distances between the main features, conformed to the golden ratio, the faces were significantly more attractive than faces with proportions based on the ratio of 1:1.5.

Although the golden ratio might be preferable to a ratio of 1:1.5, is it the ideal ratio, and is it true for every dimension? Dr Pamela M. Pallett of the Department of Psychology, University of California conducted experiments on facial attractiveness, exploring the distances between eyes and mouth and between the eyes (the 'interocular distance'). The ratios between these distances and the length or width of the face, respectively, were then calculated.

Starting with a standard colour photograph of a female face, researchers used Photoshop to vary the distance between nose and mouth by 10–50%, in steps of 10%. They then calculated the ratios as a proportion of face length. They then repeated this for nine other facial identities. During the experiment, randomly selected faces were presented two at a time on a computer screen and participants were asked to decide which face was more attractive. Paired comparison data for each original face and its ten derivations were converted to an attractiveness score on a well-established psychophysical metric for measuring attitudes (the Thurstonian scale). They found that although different faces had varying levels of attractiveness, individual attractiveness was optimal when the distance between eyes and the mouth was 36% of the face length. The relationship was curvilinear – faces at the extremes of 10% and 50% appeared grotesque. With regard to interocular distance, a similar curvilinear relationship emerged, but the optimal horizontal distance between the eyes was a different proportion of the face's width, at 46%.

Interestingly, for both ratios, the optimum figure approximated to the average face shape across all facial identities. Previous studies had also found that averaging a group of faces by computer morphing resulted in a synthetic face more attractive than any of the originals.

According to the golden ratio, the distance between eyes and the mouth should be 38% of the face length. It could be argued that the experimental figure of 36% approximates to the golden ratio, and that if a bigger sample of faces were used, it might come close. However, the ideal interocular distance was 46%, not 36% of the face width – not even close to the golden ratio. It seems that you can confirm that the golden ratio is associated with beauty only if you are selective about the dimensions you choose.

The truth is that the beauty of an object is influenced by more than just the ratio of its dimensions. If we stick with the example of the face, many other factors influence attractiveness, including symmetry, the size of the eyes and gender-specific features – a square jaw in a man, for example. Beauty is also influenced by complexion, health, facial expression and age. The golden ratio is important for some dimensions, but it is only one influence over attractiveness.

The beauty of a face is a useful illustration for the beauty of a building. Overall, the golden ratio might help to refine and improve on the attractiveness of a building's façade, but it is not necessary, nor sufficient, to guarantee its desirability. There is no single mathematical formula to create a beautiful building because beauty is influenced by site, materials, symmetry, complexity and elegance. Windows are the eyes of the building. They can be beautiful without conforming to a golden ratio – like the stained-glass windows of a gothic church. Even on a domestic scale, as we have explored, taller, narrower windows are appealing, despite the fact that their proportions do not conform to the golden ratio.

Likewise, Le Corbusier's strict adherence to his Modular system (based on the golden ratio) did not produce universally desirable results. When internal spaces conformed strictly to his system they felt rather boxy. In particular, the ceiling heights prescribed by a strict adherence to the golden ratio were suboptimal. Ceiling height is a major influence over perceived attractiveness and satisfaction.

## Ceiling height

The minimum standard for ceiling height in a new building is about 2.4 metres in the US and in Europe, and this is about average for a home, but it seems that we would prefer more headspace, literally and figuratively.

John C. Baird and colleagues published a study in the *Journal of Applied Psychology*, which was conducted on seventy-three American students. They found that preference for ceiling height in a domestic home peaked at 10 feet (3.04 metres), with preference decreasing at heights greater than this. This curvilinear relationship (the inverse U) was the same, whether they were looking at pictures of varied ceiling height or placed inside a room with a moveable ceiling. The lesson to take from this is that, on average, we would prefer our ceilings to be 60 centimetres higher than the usual standard.

Even more interesting was the effect that imagined activity in the room had on preferences. The participants wanted higher ceilings for listening to music than they did for other activities like reading, chatting and dining.

According to work conducted by Oshin Vartanian and colleagues at the University of Toronto, ceiling height is related to feelings of enclosure. Rooms with higher ceilings feel more open and approachable – people are more likely to enter them. They are also perceived to be more beautiful. These researchers went a step further by measuring brain activation. They presented images of rooms with varying ceiling heights to participants while they were in an MRI scanner. The scanner was able to pick up on changes in brain activity in real time by detecting changes in blood oxygenation. Viewing rooms with higher ceilings was associated with more activation of brain networks in the frontal and occipital lobes, which are involved in visual exploration, and thinking in three dimensions. Areas that process visual motion were activated by rooms that were judged to be more open, perhaps representing an anticipation of entering and exploring the space.

The commercial implications of this research are significant, of course. Suppose a developer wishes to build a block of flats five storeys high, with ceilings 3 metres high. Now assume that the total height of the building is fixed by the planning department. If the developers amended their plans to allow only 2.4 metres per apartment, they would be able to build a whole extra storey of flats. The implications for the homebuyer are obvious. However, investing a bit more to enjoy higher ceilings will pay dividends in mental wellbeing.

The curvilinear relationship between satisfaction and ceiling height has interesting implications for double-height, loft-style apartments. A double ceiling height is less desirable than a room 3 metres high for most people. This could be because the instinctive need for refuge is violated. We might feel rather too exposed. It is, of course, an observation that is relevant to the main living space only, because sleeping accommodation is often more enclosed. When it isn't, adaptations are often made to ensure that it is.

## Understanding the headspace of home

The things we like most about homes are the things we like most about natural landscapes. We live in a sophisticated urban culture, but psychologically and emotionally we are still living in caves. When the built environment of the city departs too much from the natural environment of our distant ancestors it becomes an instinctive, unconscious threat to our mental wellbeing. This contributes to the high rate of anxiety and depression we see in city dwellers – which we will discuss in later chapters. Environment matters.

It is not all bad news, though. We can choose homes to give us the best chance of peace and contentment, with the right balance of refuge and view, the right amount of mystery and complexity inside and out, and the right amount of exposure to nature – real or simulated.

Our home should preferably come with a garden, and/or a view of green space, but if that is not an option there are many ways to compensate. We can bring nature into the smallest of homes with indoor plants, pets or a window box. Even a simulated form of nature – a picture, or a green wall – can improve creativity and vitality while reducing stress.

Experiencing nature should not stop at your home. If you don't have a garden, you could consider taking an allotment. It's therapeutic to get your hands dirty and watch things grow. Gardening is one of the most restorative things we can do. Visit a park or an urban forest. Better still, pay a bit more rent and live by one. The less exposure you have to greenery in the city, the more important it is to get away to the countryside often. Seascapes are the most restorative, but mountains and forests are restorative too.

Our inherent curiosity has shaped our aesthetic preferences for mystery inside and outside the home: we like to do a bit of exploration in a home, just like we do in nature. Nooks and crannies are attractive, bland open spaces are not. Contrary to what modernist architects might dictate, we like some complexity and texture on the façade of a home and don't really like featureless, monochrome brick, with no balconies and decorative details to break up the frontage. With complex façades, as with landscapes, there is a limit to how much complexity we can take in before we become overloaded and confused; complexity should be under some constraint. For buildings in general we like a sense of closure, of wholeness, which comes from clear sightlines and an understanding of the whole internal space – the limits of it, its entrances and exits.

The survival instinct for refuge is balanced with the need to have a good view of the surrounding landscape. So, as much as possible, living rooms should balance the two – a view out but also a place of refuge. Windows should be tall, but not too big, and in proportion to the walls. Ceilings should not be too low. Buildings with high ceilings are inviting and inspiring.

In these chapters we have considered what features of the fabric of our homes make us content, but we have not yet touched on another very important consideration – how do we shape our homes to give them a sense of identity? What does this say about us? And, how important is it for our happiness? This is what we will turn to in the next chapter.

Part Two

# Home and Identity

It has been argued that a strong sense of self is under attack from all directions in a busy city. As we bump into different cultural groups, assumptions are challenged, affiliations change, and we are bombarded by thousands of different influences on tastes and preferences. In this environment it is perhaps even more important to have a secure place called home, which provides some consistency, some connection with the past as well as the future, and which helps us to feel centred and whole. Home is not only an important expression of identity, it also helps us to remember who we are.

For homes to make us feel centred they need to be more than just functional. They should represent our unique personalities, passions, interests and journeys through life. They should be physical manifestations of our personal biographies. While expressing who we are, they should – at the same time – *reinforce* who we are.

As Gaston Bachelard wrote in his book *The Poetics of Space*, when we are in a home of our own making, it *resonates* with us. Bachelard goes on to say that this resonance persists over time, as long as our homes reflect change and chart our journeys through life. As new interests develop, they are reflected in the home. They add to the physical biography, reinforcing a sense of progress but also a sense of continuity of self, provided markers of our roots and our past experiences remain. This sense of continuity adds to a feeling of security.

Returning to the results of my survey on the emotional value of the home, it was apparent that attachment was strongly associated with the accumulation of meaningful personal belonging and mementoes that we have accrued over the years – markers of identity. The most significant determinants of emotional attachment, in order of importance were:

- Making a big contribution to how they made their homes look
- Happy times with loved ones (kids, partner and/or friends)
- Personal belongings
- Mementos
- Inclusion in the local community

I calculated that if you were to devise an equation to determine the Emotional Added Value of a home, it would look something like this:

*Effort put in to home + Good experiences + Feeling of security – Bad times in home = Emotional Added Value*

I devised a brief questionnaire that calculates how attached you are to your home-based on the relative weighting of the most important influences. The higher the score, the higher your emotional attachment.

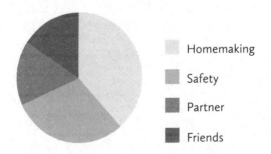

EVA Factors affecting the emotional value of your home

Therefore, an important way to preserve identity in the city is to try to have as much control as possible over where you live, how you decorate and furnish your home, who you share it with, and how you adorn it with artefacts personal to you. Let's consider these different aspects of home, and examine how city life might act as a threat to achieving these goals. In the next chapter we will explore the inherent tension between such self-expression and design.

# Chapter 5

# Status objects versus personal objects

In most homes there will be items and features that are authentically biographical and others which are there to impress – to display our 'good' taste. Some objects might be somewhere in between. For example, you might have bought a Persian rug on your travels, but know too that such a rug is fashionable.

Social scientists in the mid-twentieth century, such as Erving Goffman, observed that the communal living room was also the front room that presented its face to the public – it was a place where a certain image was portrayed. This was a hangover from the Victorian and Edwardian concepts of the reception room, where the upper middle classes received their guests. We have all retained this influence, to a greater or lesser extent, which might fight against personal expression. In other words, there is pressure to present an image to the world, rather than an authentically personal one. We are social mammals who naturally like to fit in – we want to show that we belong to a group. The extent to which we give in to this pressure will depend on the strength of our personal identity. For example, people who are less comfortable in their own skin will strive for validation from others, at the expense of their sense of self. If this extends to the home, the only resonance is the superficial resonance with what is à la mode. The home no longer reflects an authentic personal identity, but rather a more diffuse cultural and stylistic symbolism.

The recurrent trend for acquiring the correct designer products and hiding personal items takes us back to the early modernists. Minimalist interiors were promoted by Austrian architect Adolf Loos at the turn of the twentieth century in his book *Ornament and Crime.* He argued that '. . . the evolution of culture marches with the elimination of ornament from useful objects.' However, even Loos was careful to balance the idea of pure form with the need for self-expression. He related the story of a man whose architect designed everything about his home, down to the furniture and ornaments, and even their arrangement. He kept adding to and altering the layout of his home, to the point where there was nothing that the client could touch or move. What motivated this client? Was it personal fulfilment or external validation? The pattern of our lives should not be dictated by trends in decor, or by logical extension, a designer's vision of a complete home. For a home to resonate with you emotionally it should be furnished the way you want it to be, without fear of judgment. It should never give up its biographical texture.

Talya B. Rechavi, of New York's City University, examined how much people were able to personalise the more confined apartments to be found in Manhattan.

He interviewed sixteen residents about how they lived, and collected a lot of other clues, from questionnaires, photos and drawings. While the participants completed questionnaires, Rechavi made sketch drawings of the homes, paying particular attention to the various objects, pieces of furniture and memorabilia within them. He also took notes during personal tours of the living spaces.

Rechavi's research revealed that the living room had an important function in assisting the residents to have 'imaginary connections to loved ones and to events in one's life'. Particularly important objects would be gifts from loved ones and heirlooms. According to one resident, 'they remind me of the trend of my life as an adult'.

As discussed, Rechavi found that highly personal displays were in balance with the need to express an aesthetic sensibility to others – an expression of good taste. One resident went so far as to say that she tried to make a showcase out of her living room. Rechavi noted that some objects had a dual significance: while aesthetically acceptable, their personal meaning could be revealed to guests when it felt comfortable to do so.

To sum up, Rechavi's observations confirmed that the living room plays an important role in reinforcing identity through objects and experiences.

## Shared experiences

My survey revealed that personal attachment to home is not just shaped by our own hands, but by the people we share it with. We are reflected in the reactions of our peers, and, importantly, in how they shape our environment. So, a true home should embody shared experiences with others – the people who are important in our lives. It should have space to accommodate people for intimate and social intercourse, who will shape it in visible and invisible ways. Memories of them will live within the walls of our homes, for good or ill, but they are authentically a reflection of our selves.

The layout of a home can be important. When Paul Pennartz conducted detailed interviews with residents of the public housing projects in Holland, he found a clear relationship between the size of the living room and its effects on communication and experience of pleasantness. What made a living room pleasant was the orientation of furniture to encourage communication, and space for objects with some significant social meaning – mementos, heirlooms and knick-knacks.

Though much of this research feels like common sense, it is important that we never forget to connect with the different purposes of rooms. The living room a multifunctional place, used for solitary contemplation, connecting with other people through memorabilia, a place for socializing, a place for hosting family and a place where you have sex.

Rechavi's study noted that for a place to feel like a home it should contain, as a bare minimum, the 'living room prototype' – sofa, table and chair. This arrangement allows for hosting as well as intimacy. It cuts across the personal and the public, to reinforce the sense of home.

But what if space is extremely restricted, like in downtown Tokyo? In this city, and in the swelling numbers of micro-apartments in Manhattan, Seattle and Hong Kong, there is no space for the living-room prototype. In this situation, places all around the city – shopping malls, restaurants, bars, cafés – become proxies for the living room and kitchen. Also, there is very little room for personal possessions. The home has no identity of its own. Identity is expressed in the wider cityscape.

The Japanese architect Toyo Ito coined the phrase *urban nomad* to describe this phenomenon. Ito observed how urban nomads reach out for cultural icons within the city which somehow resonate with them, but he did not celebrate this. In fact, he believed that identity formed in this way was more superficial, and more at the mercy of emerging cultural trends, more external to the individual, and leaving no tangible biographical record. The cultural icons that proliferate in a city's fabric often reflect commercial rather than artistic or social memes. In this shifting and incoherent environment, identity confusion can be reinforced: leading to inconsistent relationships, insecurity, isolation, and even mental breakdown.

This is why Michael Gamble, associate professor at the Georgia Tech School of Architecture, states that we have to pay special attention to the environment surrounding a micro-home – to make sure that it responds to the needs of the inhabitant. People need somewhere to go that is restorative when they leave their apartment. 'They cannot be relegated to hanging out in a shopping mall or having to pay for a cup of coffee to use the internet.' He has found that without good public provision nearby – green space and good public buildings – there is a high risk of adverse health effects.

Some young urbanites in Manhattan appreciate that micro-apartments make it more affordable to live in a prime city-centre location, with all its facilities. However, dissatisfaction with micro-living is the norm, demonstrated by the short length of stay of most inhabitants. For example, the tiny studios in Deldridge Way, West Seattle, are often rented month to month.

They are described by residents as sterile, lonely and closet-like. Such homes might suit people in transition but should not be considered suitable places to make a home.

# Chapter 6

# Space sharing

Cities lack affordable homes to rent and so the most popular alternative to renting a micro-apartment is flat-sharing. This can be a good way of getting to know people, but it compromises how much control we have over our environment, and how much we can put our stamp on it. There is a limit to how many people we can share with and still feel that we can invite over who we want, when we want, and express our individuality.

A communal living room that is shared by many independent people often reduces sociable contact rather than increases it. Too many sharers in one house can cause people to retreat to their bedrooms. This means that the expression of identity is restricted to the bedroom.

The effect of how many people are grouped together in a building was researched in the 1970s by a study led by Andrew Baum. Researchers compared large student dormitories with smaller ones over a number of weeks. In the first three weeks, residents in the bigger dorm became 'more competitive and reactive', but by Week Seven they had mostly stopped interacting and had withdrawn in to their own rooms. In contrast, residents of the smaller dorms socialised in communal areas and were not competitive.

We retreat to private spaces when sharing with a large number of people because social encounters are hard to predict, more likely to be unwanted, and are difficult to avoid. In other words, there is less personal control over whom you have contact with and when. Ultimately, this feels threatening and uncomfortable. Over time it can cause stress-related physical and mental health problems.

A lack of control means that we might not be able to do what we want when we want – like study, cook for friends, watch TV, make a phone call or be intimate with a partner. Some activities might not be possible at all. Social crowding causes stress and physical-health complaints.

However, it is possible to design environments that can make social crowding more tolerable. A study in the *Journal of Personality and Social Psychology* looked at specific design features that would minimise stress, even with a high density of people. Researchers used scaled-down versions of rooms with different designs. Participants were then asked to place as many miniature figures in the rooms as possible without causing overcrowding. Room areas were kept constant in size but architectural features were varied – increasing the number of doors between rooms, the interruption of sightlines with staggered layouts, and the placement of partitions. All of these extra design features help to mitigate the perception of crowding and so reduce social stress.

The stress of lots of unavoidable social interactions is reduced when long corridors in student accommodation are replaced by several 'clusters' of about four rooms, each with their own communal areas. This allows smaller groups to form, who together defend their territory and agree on how to use it socially. They also have crucial 'semiprivate space', just outside the bedroom doors where people can engage superficially with what is going on in the central social space and then get more involved if they feel like it. The semiprivate space gives the feeling of a safe transition from private zones to communal areas.

As Baum observed, when safe withdrawal from a communal space into a semiprivate space is not possible, residents engage in an across-the-board withdrawal, which might persist in other situations. In an ingenious study conducted by the psychologist Leonard Bickman and colleagues, SAEs (stamped, addressed envelopes) were dropped around student dormitories of low, medium and high density. Using this lost-letter technique, the researchers could infer the amount of prosocial behaviour by observing how many letters were forwarded on to their correct destination. The number of letters returned increased as the density went down: 58% in the high-density dorm, 79% in the medium-density, and 88% in the low-density accommodation.

In smaller suite arrangements, more familiar and predictable relationships are formed and there is a greater sense of social support, which always mitigates against the stress of coming into contact with people we don't like.

When it is not possible to rearrange people in to smaller clusters there are still design interventions that can make social crowding more tolerable. A study in the *Journal of Personality and Social Psychology* created scaled-down versions of rooms and human figures. Participants were then asked to place as many miniature figures in the rooms as possible without causing overcrowding. When the researchers added partitions, or altered the number of doors between rooms, this led to a higher tolerance of crowding, as evidenced by the number of figures placed in the different rooms. Staggered layouts were much more tolerated than linear ones, because they interrupted the line of sight between people. They gave the impression of less crowding.

In summary, to create a home, and resonate with it we need the space and freedom to furnish and decorate it as we choose, display items of personal meaning and socialize with people of our choosing. However, there is a limit to how many people we can share our communal spaces with before we retreat, and the main living space no longer feels owned by anybody.

## Gardens

In overcrowded cities there is precious little room for private outside space, but if we are lucky, we can create and style our own pieces of nature. Private gardens are an extension of the home, and the emotional meaning of a private garden to its owner cannot be overstated. These external territories are defended almost as much as our interior ones.

As such, gardens are subject to the same multilayered influences as the homes to which they are attached. They contribute to a sense of place. Just as the landscaped gardens of the English country home were miniature versions of the wider countryside, customised for personal taste, so the more domestic garden is an individual's unique representation of nature. The private garden fulfils our need for nature, but it is importantly created and tended to by our own hands. It is nature filtered through our own lens, and it is all the more important for that.

Private gardens are an expression of creative endeavour and aesthetic taste but, like our living rooms, they are places for sharing, places for exploration and play and spaces for creative activity. They become imbued with piquant memories of these many activities. Urban gardening in particular is an important part of homemaking and contributes to fulfilment through multiple social meanings. While public or shared gardening has restorative and social benefits, tending our own garden has been shown to lead to the greatest levels of satisfaction.

Though much discussion around the value of expressing our unique identity seems obvious, the importance of self-expression in the fabric of the home is often ignored. To sum up what we've learnt so far, home should ideally have space for us to express our identities with objects that show our biographies, and share happy experiences in our homes with people we like. To achieve these main functions of the home, we need to have some control over the social contact we have with our housemates. In the bustle of the city we can lose a sense of who we are. Marking our territory is therefore all the more important.

# Chapter 7

# The stamp of personality

It seems inevitable that if we have the freedom to shape our homes as we see fit, it will become not only a reflection of our life experiences but something that is more fixed – our personalities. If home is an expression of us, how do different personalities effect how we design our living spaces? And, can understanding our personalities make a difference to our design choices?

Personality is an important component of our identity. It determines a lot of our preferences. Personality is a persistent pattern of thinking, feeling and behaving that develops in childhood and persists in to adulthood. It is a product of inherited temperament and formative experiences. It will stamp its mark on any home we inhabit. This begs the question – how do our personalities influence how our homes look? Will the same type of layout and living arrangement suit all of us? What effect does personality have on the balance between display objects and personal objects?

For example, someone who sets a lot of store on achieving validation from others (who scores highly on a trait known as 'agreeableness') might have a home that is more of a show home than an expression of identity. Extroverts might be more suited to living in the populous and buzzing inner city than introverts; they might prioritise sociability over solitude and privacy.

Established measures of personality might help to guide us in making the right decisions about our choices of homes and interiors, or perhaps identify why there is a mismatch. The main aim of research by the social psychologist Sam Gosling in the early 2000s was to explore the link between our personalities, measured on a scientific scale, and the character of our living spaces. His results revealed a strong influence of some personality traits in specific situations.

The measure of personality that he used was The Big Five test. It is widely accepted that most personalities can be summarised by scores on these five dimensions. If you add extra dimensions, they tend to just correlate with one or more of these. The five dimensions are:

1. Agreeableness – the degree to which you will adapt your behaviour to suit other people's wishes
2. Extroversion–introversion – the degree to which you prefer other people's company
3. Openness – the degree to which you accept and embrace difference, related to creativity
4. Emotional stability – related to neuroticism, it measures how prone you are to anxiety and low mood, and how quickly you recover from criticism, for example
5. Conscientiousness – love of process and getting the job done to the best of your ability. This will capture features of perfectionism and obsession

Gosling's team looked at two city locations for their research – the office and the student bedroom – to examine how much their 'environmental cues' could predict independent scores on the Big Five.

In the office environment, rooms of conscientious individuals were well organised, neat and uncluttered, but they were less concerned with making good use of the space. People who scored high on openness occupied distinctive and unconventional offices. Compared with the offices of introverts, those of extroverts appeared to be crafted to encourage interaction; they were relatively warm, decorated and inviting.

When the researchers looked at student bedrooms to assess personality, they had a richer set of cues to guide them. This was especially true for agreeableness, which was predicted by rooms that were cheerful, colourful, clean, organised, neat, comfortable and inviting, and which were not strewn with clothes. Raters might have assumed that pleasant people inhabit pleasant environments, or that agreeable people provide more pleasant environments for friends to visit (reflecting their sociable nature and desire to please others).

Openness was determined by the distinctiveness of the rooms, the level of decoration and the quantity or variety of books, magazines and compact discs.

As for the office environment, conscientiousness was most strongly predicted by rooms that were clean, organised and uncluttered.

Extroversion did not reliably correlate with any specific features of the personal living spaces, except for the amount of decoration. Overall, the data from student bedrooms was therefore more interesting than the office data. This was not surprising given the broader range of possibilities for self-expression in a less formal environment – a place that the students called home.

Extrapolating the findings of Gosling's research into student rooms to all living spaces offers a number of potential problems. These should be apparent to most of us. Firstly, the college years are the adult years when expressing and forming our identities are most important. We might be less free to express our personalities in our homes as we age. On the other hand, if personality is the core of identity and is largely set in childhood, we can argue that the results apply more broadly to adult life.

Secondly, any individual participating in Gosling's research knew that their living space was going to be observed for cues about their personality. So, they could have adjusted their living space to give an impression of being rather tidier or more organised than they really are, for example.

Perhaps surprisingly, it turned out that this rarely happened – or if it did happen, the changes were minor. This was determined by talking to the participants' peers, who confirmed that the rooms were pretty much the same during the experiment as they were before.

What the researchers could not determine was whether the rooms had *always* been a faux presentation of the occupants' true personality – a cover for traits that they might have perceived to be undesirable, and which they might have been railing against. In other words, the rooms could have been dominated by 'other directed identity claims'. This seems unlikely, though, given that in the first years of college we have almost unbridled freedom to express our true selves, unfettered by the watchful eyes of parents. Also, the effort required to maintain the pretence would surely be exhausting over time. It seems reasonable to assume, therefore, that our desire to express our identity is stronger than any perceived need to conform to what others might think of us.

Gosling examined the influence of personality on the micro-aspects of the internal environment, but what implications are there for inner-city homes more generally? We can probably predict that, compared to introverts, extroverts will do better in apartments as opposed to houses, prefer buzzing city-centre environments, as opposed to more suburban ones, and dwellings with more open-plan layouts compared to more encapsulated ones. They should prefer homes with less emphasis on privacy and more emphasis on socialising.

On an even bigger scale, it might be predicted that extroverts who score highly on openness to experience would prefer more diverse neighbourhoods within cosmopolitan cities than those who are less open. Introverts and conscientious types are likely to value the peace and quiet of more private and secluded homes.

There has been some research attempting to make a definitive link between the Big Five traits and our preferences for certain home designs. A study by Nils Myszkowski and Martin Storme, of the Université Paris Descartes, looked at how the Big Five traits affect our appreciation of, and response to, product design. It is interesting to speculate on the implications of their findings when it comes to assessing the design of someone's home.

The researchers asked mostly female students to complete the Big Five Inventory and a questionnaire called the Centrality of Visual Product Aesthetics (CVPA), which measures the salience of visual design in a consumer's relationships with products. Salience includes how much an individual values design in products, their skill in assessing the quality of the design, and how much an appealing design would urge the individual to buy the product. As the authors point out, 'One may value design but may not necessarily feel competent at identifying superior design. Likewise, one may value design but may not feel the urge of buying products with a superior design.'

The biggest determinant of scores on the CVPA was the Openness to Experience score on the Big Five. However, the direction of effect was the opposite to what we might intuitively predict: openness was negatively correlated with the CVPA score. The researchers suggest 'High Openness individuals may tend to focus more inquisitively on other aspects of products, leading them to disregard aesthetic characteristics.' In other words, such individuals are not superficial. They might be less impressed by a well-dressed show home, for example, than by its layout, its location and its potential as a place for having new experiences.

Another interesting finding was that highly agreeable personalities were more likely to value visual aesthetics, in contrast to the High Openness personalities. As discussed above, Agreeableness is about fitting in. It's about 'people pleasing'. So, in their minds, owning the product is about increasing their social desirability. In other words, being overly concerned with the material appearance of a home relates to a need for external, rather than internal, validation. It could be argued that trend-setting areas of a city magnify this effect.

## Myers-Briggs

Occupational psychologists and HR consultants the world over know about the Myers-Briggs personality test. Some research has been conducted that reveals associations between the results of this test and home layouts. Based on the work of Carl Jung, the test allocates you to one of four dichotomous choices:

1. Extroversion versus introversion
   *Most of us are very familiar with these terms. Extroverts crave company, while introverts tend towards a need for solitude and quiet contemplation.*
2. Sensing versus intuiting
   *Sensing personalities are characterised by a desire for concrete information so that they can make rational choices. Intuiting personalities tend to be more open to abstract concepts.*
3. Thinking versus feeling
   *Thinking personality types are more detached from their emotions and highly methodical and logical in their approach to decision making, but not necessarily concrete in their thinking. Feeling types are empathic and people-oriented.*
4. Judging versus perceiving
   *Judging types like situations to be settled and resolved. Perceiving types are happy to live with more ambiguity.*

Associate Professor Carl Matthews and his colleagues, of the School of Architecture, University of Texas, examined the design preferences of ninety-one interior-design students by asking them to design their own ideal home. Correlations between their design preferences and relative scores on each of the four Myers-Briggs dimensions (for example, strong extrovert or strong introvert) were examined.

Extroverts, as was predicted *a priori*, exhibited a preference for more direct access into rooms and less separation between public and private spaces. A typical extrovert design would have a lot of glass in the external walls (a high void to solid ratio), and hence be much more open to the world. There would be fewer full-height partitions, bathrooms would open on to bedrooms, and bedrooms would open on to living spaces. Storage cupboards would be tucked away to allow more lines of sight through the interior.

In contrast, introverts tended to prefer indirect entry into the living area (via a hallway or lobby) and more full-height boundaries between rooms. They preferred external walls with a lower void to solid ratio: windows were an opportunity to 'overlook life' rather than be exposed to it.

Sensing personalities, with their desire for concrete information, had a preference for order, symmetry and grid-based layouts (internal and external). Texture was less important – perhaps regarded as too messy.

The influence of more free-thinking, intuiting personalities on design preferences was more nuanced. Scores on this dimension predicted a preference for designs with more texture – such as the use of textured concrete, and a circuitous stairway entrance to the home. Intuitives favoured 'secret places' which revealed themselves only gradually, or through peepholes, perhaps reflecting a more romantic, explorative approach to living.

Thinking personality types, with their cold, logical approach to life, preferred more rational, symmetrical designs, with grid-based layouts and exteriors. They tended to avoid interior openness and colour warmth. Entrances were transitional.

Empathic, feeling types preferred more open layouts and direct entrance arrangements, like the extroverts.

Their inherent interest in other people, as well as their emotional intelligence, drew them to more social environments. They specifically had a preference for warmer colours, like creams, tans, browns and subtle greens.

Judging types, with their dislike of ambiguity, preferred separation of public and private spaces, but less rigidly than the introverts. Not surprisingly, they also had a preference for order and grid – a design that is immediately understandable, and therefore more resolved in the mind.

Finally, perceiving personality types who can tolerate a degree of uncertainty, and can see both points of view, were more likely to include half open walls, and a freer, more open layout. In other words, they were drawn to features that might be regarded as unresolved. They were also happy with more exposure to the outside world.

The conclusions of this study seem intuitively correct, but they should be treated with some caution. It is not stated in the research report that the assessors of the design preferences (faculty supervisors) were blind to the students' personalities.

Interpreting the results required a judgment based on the relative importance of scores on the various dimensions. The design preferences clearly overlapped on many of the dimensions. For example, preferences were similar for sensing, thinking and judging types. This might reflect a problem with the personality test itself. The distinctiveness of the different dimensions is questionable. The process of fitting people into different categories has been shown to be unreliable (both between raters and for the same rater on different occasions).

Nevertheless, this sort of research is illuminating, and might help guide the choices we make when deciding where to live and how to live in the city. Personality tests might also guide architects and designers. It is the job of architects and designers to really understand their client's needs and desires, and personality tests might help in this process. When we are searching for a suitable home, some self-tests might kick start the process of deciding what we really want from it.

## Kelly's repertory grid

Given that personality tests alone are unlikely to be sufficient to match us to our best environments, more detailed methods of personal analysis might be useful to complement them. The influential American psychologist George Kelly reasoned that we all see the world through a unique lens, and that we can be our own psychologists in examining what this lens consists of. In his Repertory Grid Technique, participants can choose their own parameters in determining their ideal home.

The process goes like this: once we have decided on the topic – in this case our ideal home – we define the *elements.* In this case the elements, taken together, can give a profound insight into pictures of the inside of various styles of home, which are used to determine our preferences. Then we chose subjective constructs on which to rate these elements. They are always expressed as a contrast, and can be rated on a scale of our choice (e.g. from -8 to +8).

In the experiment, pictures of rooms were defined by a particular individual – let's say Person A – in terms of *crowded* or *spacious, simple* or *finicky, natural* or *stylistic, plain* or *elaborate, heavy* or *light, coordinated* or *uncoordinated, comfortable* or *uncomfortable, specific* or *free, formal* or *informal* and *oppressive* or *unoppressive.*

Person A did not have to fit a personality type. What was interesting is how the constructs chosen by that indivdual all relate to one another. Suppose that Person A felt oppressed (and uncomfortable) in a place that is formal, stylised or overly elaborate (elaborate being closely related to stylistic and finicky). Other features that made Person A feel oppressed and uncomfortable, but less so, were a room that was crowded, 'heavy' in appearance, and with little flexibility of function.

No two people choose the same constructs, nor exhibit the same emotional responses to the same pictures. Person B might rate the pictures on the constructs *happy* or *sad, bright* or *dark, tidy* or *cluttered, inspiring* or *deflating*, and so on. This would be no less valid, and arguably more informative, than the Big Five or the Myers-Briggs tests. The constructs that we choose provide important insights into our unique aesthetic and architectural preferences. If we can nail these down, we can have more control over where we live, and how are homes are designed, and this could help us to live happier lives.

Chapter 8

# Tailor-made homes

Presuming that we know what we are like, informed by a good knowledge of who we are, we might conclude that, to be perfectly happy in a home, we should design it ourselves. Olivier Marc argued, in his book *Psychology of the House*, that the most aesthetically pleasing and most psychologically healthy built environment is one that emerges organically from the efforts of local people, serving their own needs and using materials sourced from their own location.

According to Mike Hardwick, a project manager and self-build expert for the National Self Build & Renovation Centre, 'Developer-built houses are not necessarily poor products ... but they're often disappointing places [in which] to live.' If you self-build, you can take control of the design, and create a home that suits your lifestyle or which can adapt to changes in your circumstances in the future. Not only that, but the home will have a much stronger sense of place. Embedded within its masonry will be the identity of the person or persons who made it.

There are many other good examples of self-build developments around the world. Stockholm's council has had a self-build department for almost a century. The senate in Berlin has an office that not only promotes self-build but also offers practical help: the office has links to banks that finance the projects. In Berlin, self-build is regarded as particularly low risk, because of the personal investment involved. Why would anyone default on their loan if it meant that they would lose a home towards which they have such a strong sense of ownership? People who self-build need the project to succeed not just for their own welfare but for strong emotional and social reasons. There is a resource benefit too. In all cases, self-builds not only cut the cost of building, thereby providing more housing in cities where this is in short supply, but they nearly always lead to a greater sense of ownership of home and neighbourhood.

On the other hand, new-build homes lack a sense of history, which adds much to a sense of place, and of homeliness. Another problem is that building your own home is stressful. It is hard to keep track of costs, and the number of decisions can be almost overwhelming. Perhaps these issues explain why so many self-builders sell up not long after they have finally moved into the finished project. The irony is that the longer you live in a home, the more it develops character; it becomes a home and its inhabitants can form attachments to it.

There are, however, examples of good housing projects that are based on a self-build principle but guided or facilitated by the architect. A much-celebrated example is the housing community in Lewisham, southeast London, comprising Walters Way, Segal Close and Greenstreet Hill. It was conceived by the German architect Walter Segal, who provided outline designs and low-cost off-the-peg materials for simple, wooden-framed houses. The residents were consulted on the final designs, and then went ahead and built them. All they needed to do was learn how to saw in a straight line and how to drill a straight hole. Other self-builders in the community stepped in when things got tricky – when needing to raise up a wall, for example.

The journalist Alice Grahame wrote about her experience of the site in an article for the *Guardian* newspaper. The personal contribution to varying styles of houses was apparent: 'The 13 half-timbered boxes are routinely mistaken for prefabs, an artists' colony, Swiss chalets, eco-houses, a kibbutz, Scandinavian holiday cabins, Jamaican beach houses – or even a Japanese temple.'

The Quinta Monroy development, by the Chilean architect Alejandro Aravena, won the prestigious Pritzker Architecture Prize. His novel approach was to construct 'half a house' at an affordable price, which the owners could then finish off gradually, as money allowed. Although conceived as a low-cost, social housing project, it had the added benefit of allowing owners to shape their homes as they saw fit, increasing the sense of ownership.

Most of us do not have the opportunity to build our own homes – especially in cities where land is scarce – and finding the ideal home to match our needs is equally challenging. The options remaining are (a) to adapt spaces that at first glance seem unsuitable or (b) to buy city homes that have flexibility 'designed in'.

## (A) ADAPTING BUILDINGS

I've already touched on how Londoners have changed the internal layouts of their homes to become more engaged with their gardens, but repurposing can happen on a larger scale.

Erno Goldfinger's Balfron Tower is a high-rise tower in east London, originally conceived as good-quality social housing. Keen to demonstrate the quality and livability of his high-rise homes, Goldfinger himself lived in the tower block for a while. Mistakes were made, which were typical of the time: the entrance was not sufficiently secure and there was no concierge on-site. Crime and vandalism became commonplace in the communal areas that were open to the street. There was not enough money spent on maintenance. Decades later the tower was inhabited by young designers paying 'social rent', who adapted their flats in their own style and in response to how they felt about the building. They were, in effect, artists in residence.

The alternative Freetown Christiania community in Copenhagen is regarded as a success by some and a blight by others. It was set up forty-five years ago by squatters in an old military base. Drug-taking is commonplace, and although officially illegal, prohibition is not enforced provided it does not spill out into the wider community. The main drag is called Pushers Street. When I visited, it seemed to be mostly cannabis that was being sold and consumed.

Shops sell forty different types of hashish. This seemed to be one of the main attractions for visitors, in common with the coffee shops of Amsterdam. It is a self-governing commune of 900 occupants, including anarchists, artists and hippies, and has stood the test of time. Many are third-generation 'immigrants' in a zone proudly proclaiming itself to be outside the European Union.

Writing in *Vanity Fair* in 2013, the journalist Tom Freston celebrated the vitality and ingenuity of its residents, who have now bought most of Christiania from the government, as part of a cooperative: 'Christiania has grown up to be a cool, verdant little village in a corner of Copenhagen. I had underestimated the work ethic and the diligence of the Danes. They have built an entire settlement of spare, humble, Hobbit-like homes that surrounds a lake and runs along gravel paths and cobblestone roads that wind through woods to the seaside. Older buildings have been restored and are often covered in murals. There are bars, cafés, grocery shops, a huge building-supply store, a museum, art galleries, a concert hall, a skateboard park, a recycling center, even a recording studio (inside a shipping container).'

What has made Christiana successful has been the government decision to sell the buildings (which were valuable government assets) at way below market value, to residents who kept the communal spirit alive: individual ownership is not allowed. Residents own shares in the whole cooperative. Sadly, no such arrangement has been made for the artists who carved out their live–work units from unused warehouses and factories in Hackney Wick and Fish Island in east London. These are now encroached on all sides by the powers of regeneration (alternatively known as gentrification), and rents are increasing and developers moving in. As this trend creeps across London and many other cities, the artists and creatives seeking cheap rents are forced out of the very areas that they have made more desirable.

## (B) FLEXIBLE HOMES

We have considered how the appearance and structure of a healthy home should resonate with our identity in order for us to feel optimally content and grounded. We also looked at how the home should evolve as we do, so that this resonance isn't lost over time. The book *Evolutionary*

*Architecture* by Eugene Tsui suggests that the ideal home should be like a living organism, responding to changing spatial and functional needs as in nature. So, as the shell grows with the snail, floors, walls and roofs need not enclose us in static boxes but rather adapt to our changing needs. These second skins can, with some ingenuity, move in many different ways – contracting, expanding, covering, uncovering, swivelling, folding, unfolding. Perhaps the biggest contribution that architecture can make to human happiness is to design increasingly flexible houses that we can change as we see fit.

The Rietveld Schröder House, Utrecht

The Rietveld Schröder House in Utrecht was built in 1924 by Dutch architect Gerrit Rietveld for Mrs Truus Schröder- Schräder and her three children. It was probably the first truly flexible home, one that Mrs Schröder-Schräder wanted ideally to be free of internal walls. In fact, the whole living area is a dynamic, changeable zone. The space can be used open, or subdivided in an endless number of ways by a system of sliding and revolving panels. When entirely partitioned in, the living level comprises three bedrooms, bathroom and living room. In between this and the open state is an endless series of permutations, each providing its own spatial experience. So, depending on whether you're an artist, a popular party host or a traditional family, the building can be customised to suit. It can be as cluttered or as uncluttered as you like. Different parts could be used to suit the needs of different people under the same roof.

This was not a fanciful architectural dead end. Many modernist homes built in the next three decades incorporated some form of flexibility. The concrete-frame technology made this increasingly possible. Pillars held up the structure, not the walls. If a wall is not needed to hold up a building, it can be added and removed at will.

Walter Segal's cleverly designed modular prefabs on Walters Way were highly flexible. None of the walls were weight-bearing in themselves, and could be bolted on or removed as necessary. Segal strongly believed that a house should adapt to its occupants, not the other way round. The post and beam design meant that rooms could be enlarged and extensions added easily and affordably. So, if a family were to grow, for example, rooms could be added or widened.

## Individual versus architect

The major crime of modernist architecture, and its perpetual legacy, is that it too often dictates how we should live. Although some modern homes are designed with flexibility in mind, most are not. The unadorned home that is so revered by so many fails to resonate with and thereby reinforce a healthy sense of self. The minimalist building is not so much a home as a show home, sacrificing individual identity to the ego of the architect.

We have a choice about whether we live in an impoverished box or something richer, something more textured and personal. Perhaps it is time to heed the words of an editorial written some sixty years ago in the journal *House Beautiful*, entitled 'Threat to the Next America'. This told the story of a 'highly intelligent, now disillusioned, woman who spent more than $70,000 building a 1-room house that is nothing but a glass cage on stilts.' This was widely believed to be a reference to Edith Farnsworth. It chillingly concluded, 'Two ways of life stretch before us. One leads to the richness of variety, to comfort and beauty. The other, the one we want fully to expose to you, retreats to poverty and unlivability. Worst of all, it contains the threat of cultural dictatorship.'

When it comes to minimalist glass boxes, it might be better to regard them as sculptures rather than homes. Much like Mies van der Rohe's Barcelona Pavilion, they are buildings for exhibiting rather than inhabiting.

## Understanding the headspace of home identity

This section has been all about how much a home can give back to us if we put effort into making it a reflection of who we are and who we choose to share it with. Choice is key. If you have no control over who shares your home, you tend to retreat from social contact altogether, and give up on ownership of the place you inhabit. If your home is so small that it can't accommodate a sofa, table and chair, it is not going to make you happy.

The upward pressure on rents in a busy city can mean that we compromise on space or privacy, or both. It is important to have some constancy. Short-term lets are bad for the soul. Personality has a part to play in shaping a home's identity, and shaping our preferences for different types of home – layout, and degree of exposure to the street. Where possible, we should choose a home that suits our personality, or customise it to fit.

It is important for us to have more of a say on design and architecture – architects should not dictate how we live. It should be the other way around. Identity is about distinctiveness, and a sense of place. In the next section we will explore how neighbourhoods can gain a sense of place, to which we then become attached. Attachment makes it more likely that we will contribute to the neighbourhood by building its social and cultural capital – ideas that we will explore in the next chapter.

# Part Three

# Neighbourhood

We have learnt about what factors make for a good home: a balance between cave-like refuge and a view of nature; a need for complexity and mystery as opposed to bland minimalism; a need for some order and completeness to constrain that complexity; possibilities for personal expression; the space to share your home with people of your choosing; and a good fit between the physical aspects of your home and your culture and personality.

However, as we have seen when discussing the communities of Christiania and Walters Way, the places we inhabit cannot be separated from their context – the local community. To what extent can we extend the psychology of the home to the psychology of the neighbourhood? Experience suggests that the need for security, visual interest and issues of distinctive identity (a sense of place) extend beyond the home. The healthy home acts as a venue to bring loved ones together. It is a social space. When scaled up to the local community, what influences bring people together and what influences drive people apart? Good neighbourhoods have social capital; they provide the buzz of human activity and a feeling of connectedness that we all crave in order to live happy lives.

Cities are so vast that we tend to restrict most of our movements to the local neighbourhood, and when they work well, cities are a collection of villages. A close-knit neighbourhood acts as an antidote to the sometimes uncaring wider cityscape. This is all the more important in very busy cities, because they tend to be more impersonal when you travel outside of your own community. The busier the city, the more unhelpful others can be. For example, in an old study conducted before mobile phones, researchers knocked on people's doors in distress, asking if they could use their landlines. Homeowners were more likely to be obliging in rural Massachusetts than in the dense city of Boston. In another study, researchers rang random members of the public in Chicago, New York and Philadelphia from an old call box, saying that they misdialled but had run out of credit. More people offered to redial the correct number for them and pass on a message in the lower-density cities. Another method looked at how often people returned the balance of accidental overpayments for services. There was a marked difference in small towns (80 per cent) compared to cities (55 per cent).

Large cities suffer from 'bystander apathy'. Residents are less likely to rush to the assistance of others who are in trouble, although this is complicated by the effect of tensions between different peer groups or different ethnic groups. Sometimes people fear that when someone is being attacked the aggression will be directed at them. This is not an unreasonable fear. However, there are many cases that are not threatening but where assistance is needed: people are simply injured, desperate for food or shelter, or intending to injure themselves.

One mediating factor is the increased speed at which people walk in dense cities, perhaps due to the pressure of other people when trying to move around and the sense of a faster pace of life. Bystander apathy and aloofness is a way of coping with both a particularly urban form of sensory overload (which increases fatigue and irritability) and the stress of other people getting in the way of our progress and thwarting some goal or other (getting to the theatre, shopping or simply getting home in time to be with the children). When there is competition for a place on a train or some other shared goal, this can quite rapidly lead to irritation, conflict and even aggression.

We can cope with familiar places and people, but unwanted and frequent intrusions by strangers on our homeward journeys are particularly stressful. Other strangers are therefore shrugged off as a protective mechanism. It is perhaps not surprising that we screen out such interference, learning to focus only on interactions that personally affect our wellbeing. Overall, people are simply more willing to assist strangers in less crowded places because they are free of urban overload.

Given all these urban influences that have the potential to push us apart, we must consider carefully the neighbourhood where we choose to live, where its beating heart lies, and how we can make the most of it. Research shows us that being near a thriving main street is crucially important.

Chapter 9

# Street life

Two-thirds of Londoners live no more than 500 metres from a main street, and this is probably true of most large cities that evolved before the car. The eminent architectural psychologist Christopher Alexander wrote that the further you live from a main street, the less happy you tend to be. The main street is the artery pumping through the city neighbourhood, which should keep the local community alive. It is a route to the rest of the city, and, in turn, it brings visitors from other parts of the city. Ideally, it is where locals and visitors meet in mutually beneficial ways – commercial, social and cultural.

It can be a pleasure in itself just to walk along a city's vibrant streets with no purpose in mind, passing outside your own locality and into others, taking in the varied sights, sounds and smells of human activity. The French writer Charles Baudelaire was enamoured by the romantic notion of an aimless, recreational pedestrian, a person whom he called a *flâneur*. According to Cornelia Skinner, in her book *Elegant Wits and Grand Horizontals*, the *flâneur* is 'unencumbered by any obligation or sense of urgency with the leisurely discrimination of a gourmet, savouring the multiple flavours of his city'. The American film-maker and writer Susan Sontag embraced the concept, encouraging us all to cruise 'the urban inferno the landscape of voluptuous extremes'.

Jane Jacobs, an American-Canadian journalist, became a famously strident defender of the traditional terraced main street, at a time when it was most under threat – after the Second World War. The new war, especially fierce in the 1950s and 1960s but continuing right up to the present day, was the war against mass demolition of streets in the name of urban regeneration. She became one of the most influential critics of urban planning in the last century, despite having no formal training in town planning or architecture. This fact, and the fact that she was a woman fighting against the male-dominated orthodoxy of the time, provoked a fiercely negative reaction.

This did not stop her book *The Death and Life of Great American Cities*, written in 1961, from sending shockwaves through the profession. According to Herbert Muschamp, the chief architecture critic of *The Times*, it was 'one of 20th-century architecture's most traumatic events'.

The book was a reaction to political pressure to bulldoze run-down neighbourhoods in order to engineer cleaner ones, with more light and air. The prevailing wisdom was to knock down terraced 'slums' and then build tower blocks with more space around them. Jacobs fought tooth and nail to impress upon councils the importance of main streets in keeping local neighbourhoods alive, and she did not shy away from direct action. In 1961 she was removed, with other screaming protestors, from a City Planning Commission hearing on the regeneration of Greenwich Village in Manhattan. Her campaign successfully saved it from a 'slum clearance' programme.

In 1968, she was arrested on charges of second-degree riot and criminal mischief after disrupting a public meeting on the construction of the Lower Manhattan Expressway, which would have cut right through Soho and Little Italy. Once again, she was successful in stopping a plan that would have irreversibly divided and dispersed these communities. Jacobs had witnessed a decade earlier how neighbourhoods could wither and die at the mercy of a planner's misguided dream of regeneration and renewal. While working in a planning department as a secretary, she had studied the effects of the redevelopment of housing blocks in Philadelphia by the architect Edmund Bacon. When Bacon provided her with a tour of his work, she was shocked to discover that, when compared to the undeveloped blocks, his 'development' had killed off virtually all life on the street. 'Impersonal streets', she would later write, 'make impersonal people.'

Main streets should allow for varied commercial and leisure activities, run by members of the community to serve the local community. In this way they stamp an identity and sense of place on an area. The factors that make a house a home apply also to making a place a neighbourhood, and the building block of the neighbourhood is the street, no matter how untidy it might sometimes become.

## Beautiful chaos – diversity in the street

Jacobs admired the 'strips of chaos' that made up parts of East Harlem, which had a 'weird wisdom of their own', unplanned and organic, meeting the needs of the community. Her obituary in the *New York Times* states that 'Ms Jacobs's thesis was supported and enlarged by her deep, eclectic reading. But most compelling was her description of the everyday life she witnessed from her home above a candy store at 555 Hudson Street.' This was her evocative description, taken from *The Death and Life of Great American Cities*:

> She puts out her garbage, children go to school, the drycleaner and barber open their shops, housewives come out to chat, longshoremen visit the local bar, teenagers return from school and change to go out on dates, and another day is played out. Sometimes odd things happen: a bagpiper shows up on a February night, and delighted listeners gather around. Whether neighbors or strangers, people are safer because they are almost never alone.

When we say that lively streets reflect a community, what we are talking about is social capital – another term coined by Jacobs. People need people in order to thrive as individuals. It is only through community relationships that we exist at all, and for this we need a certain kind of street life. Through erudition and research on the ground, she determined the ingredients that were needed. These were the four main generators of the successful street:

1. Mixed uses – Streets should serve a variety of functions, causing people to come and go at different times, to keep street life going, and to maintain 'eyes on the street' but to come together in some communal places. So, lively streets should contain a mixture of high-end shops, shops for basic goods, cafés, bars, garages, restaurants, museums and so on. They should be a mixture of form and function. They should provide high-end culture and at the same time provide people with

things that they actually need, as opposed to a row of useless gentrified boutiques. People should not be separated by overhead walkways and alleyways but be encouraged to walk the streetscape and mingle.

2. Small blocks –'Most blocks should be short,' Jacobs said, and the opportunities for turning corners frequent. Diverse flows of human traffic occur on a human scale and increase the chance to mingle.

3. Aged buildings – Jacobs argued that knocking down old buildings should be resisted for economic reasons. Having studied the economy of cities at length, she had noticed how new buildings had to pay for their own construction costs, making their rents often unaffordable for the average resident or small business. Old buildings, she argued, might be dilapidated, but they were paid off and were more accessible to the fledgling businesses, artists and young people that are essential for keeping a neighbourhood vital.

4. A minimum concentration of people – Without enough people living by a street, it cannot thrive. Relocating people to distant tower blocks, or cutting up a community with an expressway, will kill off a street.

All four generators work together to make our streets and districts vital and interesting.

More recently, Dr Suzanne Hall of the London School of Economics studied how all four factors played a part in the street life of the more ethnically diverse areas of London between 2000 and 2006. She noted that while small independent shops had substantially declined across the UK as a whole (due to the trend for driving to superstores and buying on the Internet), this was not the case in ethnically diverse areas of London, where there had been a 78.5 per cent increase in independent shops over those six years. While diversity appeared to be driving the growth, she wanted to know more about the mechanisms. One of her case studies was Rye Lane in Peckham, South London. She noticed that the key to its livelihood was the opportunity for micro-economies, using flexible terms of rental and sub-letting arrangements. She noted: '25% of shops on Rye Lane had subdivided into smaller shops, and rentals ranged from prices per chair per week in the case of hair and nail salons, to a wide variety of flat rates per square meter.' Having multiple sublets within the same building not only allowed for fledgling businesses to gain a foothold, it also allowed for a kind of cross-fertilisation. For example, a survey by Western Union revealed that 75 per cent of customers making A Western Union Money Transfer transaction also purchased other products, and 47 per cent of people visit a shop more often once they know that Western Union is available at the store.

So, it is evident that Rye Lane has the generators of growth and community that Jacobs outlined. Individuals who are just starting out in business inhabit plots at low rent, giving them room to grow, and there is a sufficient density of customers afforded by ongoing population flux. The uses are mixed because the people are mixed in demographics and ethnicity, and the individual shops are small and personal. Rye Lane thrives because of its diversity.

Dr Hall observed that good public transport was key to the economic prosperity of a neighbourhood. Walworth Road in south London, for example, had eighteen buses an hour pass through it. Although it is not an affluent area, the weekly expenditure on the street rivalled that of the affluent Hampstead High Street, because of the density of the population living along it, and the extensive public transport. The use of pop-up shops in vacant commercial lots fostered experimentation and interest – it enriched the street life while also incubating new business.

## Complexity within order, again

A street with diverse uses will inevitably have a diverse appearance. There have been a number of investigations examining the revitalising effects of visiting a street with a diverse aesthetic. In a lab-based study, 145 digitally generated images of streets were created with variations in their physical attributes, including roofline silhouettes, surface ornamentation and the number of storeys to a building. In a web-based survey, 263 participants then rated the streetscapes in terms of how much they might feel emotionally restored by spending time there.

The perceived restorative effects increased with increasing variation in each building overall and with increasing variation in the ornament of the façades. On the other hand, taller buildings had a negative emotional effect. Human scale was important. Emotional restoration also depended on ratings of fascination with the street, and the degree of contrast with a participant's own neighbourhood (the feeling of being away). So, a variation in the appearance of a street, but within certain height constraints, makes us happier. A case once again of complexity within order. Shopping malls increasingly try to recreate the medieval square (albeit Vegas-style).

The evolutionary psychologist Steven Pinker has argued that the modernist distaste for ornament on and in our homes ignores our instinctive preference for the texture and complexity seen in nature. In his book *The Blank Slate* he devotes a page to urban design, and states, 'The belief that human tastes are reversible cultural preferences has led social planners to write off people's enjoyment of ornament, natural light and human scale and force millions of people to live in drab cement boxes.' There is perhaps another unconscious influence at work: we also seem to prefer buildings that display evidence of the human hand in their creation. A street that has evolved over centuries, containing a variety of architectural styles from different ages, and evidence of the craft of artisans, has far more visual appeal than a drab office block or a monochrome housing development.

Inevitably, modern streets need to be built as cities expand or repurpose disused areas. Since the turn of the millennium there have been attempts to encourage visual variety when there is no history to draw upon. One often-quoted example is the Sporenburg project in Amsterdam. Owners bought a standard plot on the terraced street and within the constraints of a fixed height and width and depth they then employed a designer to customise their home to suit their own functional and aesthetic preferences, leading to a wide variety of internal orientations, openings and façades. The result was a street full of variation and human interest but with dimensions dictated by identical housing plots – complexity within order. This freedom of individual expression was the antithesis of the one-size-fits-all solution to urban planning promoted by modernists.

Sporenburg houses, Amsterdam

The other simple way to make a street more visually interesting is to plant trees and shrubs. Not only do they satisfy our need for a fix of nature, they add variety and complexity, breaking up the streetscape. There are many interesting studies on the effect of trees on the visual appeal of a street, and their calming effects. These are usefully summarised by Professor Emeritus Richard C. Smarsdon, of the College of Environmental Science and Forestry, Syracuse, New York. When comparing paired images of urban scenes that are similar except for the presence or absence of vegetation, the former are rated as more pleasant. Trees have a visual appeal due to their fractal shapes, and their leaves of varied colours and ever-changing appearance, filtering and reflecting the light. They are a soft counterpoint to hard landscaping, but they also seem to add emphasis to buildings: buildings with trees framing them are recalled better (in terms of their defining features) than those without. The greenery increases their salience in two ways – it makes them more noticeable and more attractive. The added value of trees is particularly important for residential streets. Smarsdon himself discovered that adding vegetation to a street had a much greater impact on visual appeal than improving building façades or adding street furniture. It can break up otherwise monotonous lines of buildings, or punctuate façades that compete in jarring ways. Taller and broader trees are preferred over squat ones with a small spread. We like a density of about one tree per house: if the street becomes too crowded with vegetation it loses its appeal – it is as if nature is taking over, obscuring too much of the view.

Planting strips between pavements and streets also greatly improves the appeal of a street, acting as buffer zones between pedestrians and traffic.

## Walkability

Stronger evidence for the preference for interesting streets can be determined by judgments on 'walkability' – how much people are willing to walk along a street rather than take a car. Hieronymus C. Borst and colleagues, based in Delft, Holland, investigated relationships between street characteristics and perceived walkability, as reported by elderly people. Some 288 independently-living older people between 55 and 80 years old were asked to assess different segments of a street. The more walkable segments were lined with trees and front gardens. They also had good pedestrian crossings, low traffic volumes, parks, good public transport, and lots of shops, cafés, bars and restaurants. Borst showed that a high density of flats, high-rise buildings and the presence of litter would deter a journey by foot.

Determinants of a street's walkability could be boiled down to four main factors: scenic appeal, including a variety of façades, and as much greenery as possible; tidiness; the buzz of human activity; and buildings on a human scale.

At the other end of the life cycle, these same features of the street make parents feel more assured of their children's safety when walking around the neighbourhood. In a study conducted by Sarah Foster of the University of Western Australia, parents were most likely to perceive a safer neighbourhood when there were features that encouraged pedestrians while minimising vehicle traffic. She concluded that the 'natural surveillance' generated by a more walkable neighbourhood may help alleviate parents' fears about strangers.

The general layout of the network of streets can help to facilitate a more walkable network. Interestingly, the grid system is preferable to the more tortuous layouts of many suburbs, which fan out like arteries and capillaries. Within the 'short blocks' advocated by Jane Jacobs, the more active, dense, street life gives children more supervision. In contrast, suburban children begin their walks to school along quiet, meandering roads, starting off in cul-de-sacs, but later in their journeys they are forced onto busy arterial roads. Not only is this road layout less direct, it is not as well supervised, and involves getting in close proximity to a lot of traffic.

Jonathan Gallimore of Utah University determined that the grid system was preferable because it provided a more direct route, but their streets were also considered more walkable by parents and children alike. There was a perception that crime was rarer, perhaps because there were more eyes on the streets. The streets of the urban grid were also perceived to be more inclusive of minorities because of their greater diversity, and so felt less threatening. All these factors resulted in more eleven-year-old (fifth grade) children walking to school in the new grid-based city neighbourhoods.

Another feature of grid systems is that the speed of the traffic might be more easily controlled than in an arterial system. The parents in the study were also of the opinion that streets busy with traffic could be more easily avoided with a short detour.

An interesting study carried out in Texas suggested that if the sides of roads were more landscaped, with green verges, trees and so on, there were fewer accidents. Motorists appear to use trees in order to properly gauge their speed. Traffic engineers in France were concerned that the traditional lines of plane trees signalling the approach to a town were associated with an increase in fatal collisions. It turns out that this is not confirmed by the scientific evidence. The trees are, in fact, likely to make cars slow down. Green verges on roads might make drivers reduce their speed, because they make them feel calmer. The implication is that by finding ways to green up the sides of our roads we can make them more walkable on two counts – the direct restorative value of nature, and the secondary benefit of more subdued traffic.

Kazunori Hanyu, at Nihon University, Tokyo, asked twenty-four participants to look for twelve visual properties in a series of neighbourhood scenes while also rating their emotional responses to the scenes. He then looked at correlations between them, and drew out the relationships that seemed to group together – a process called 'canonical variance'. Scenes with 'naturalness, openness and complexity' were perceived as particularly pleasant, safe and relaxing, but they were also interesting, exciting and active. When the amount of traffic was increased in the scenes, the emotional reactions were less positive. Excitement, interest and a bit of fear were invoked by scenes with complexity, lack of coherence, non-uniform lighting and some mystery caused by hidden places. So the desire for mystery is apparent not just in natural landscape, or the internal layout of a home, but also in the streetscape. We like the process of discovering buildings obscured by nature.

Further evidence for this is provided by Masatake Ikemi at Nihon University in Tokyo, who conducted a study of preference for building façades that were open, or obscured partly by trees. Participants were presented with twelve photomontages of housing façades that were situated between two trees, and were asked to express their preference. In the high-mystery condition, the two edges of the house were completely concealed, while in the low-mystery condition most of the edges could be seen through the leaves. There was a middle-mystery condition that was between the two. They found that the high-mystery conditions were the most preferred, by a wide margin. They also found that a more novel façade increased the preference even more.

Street art has long been a way of improving visual interest on a street. According to Yui Motoyama and Kazunori Hanyu, also at Nihon University, sculptures of natural subjects that are perceived as pleasant will make an urban landscape feel more pleasant also. In a comparison between a ladybird sculpture and a sculpture of a spider, the former, not the latter, was perceived to increase the pleasantness of the street.

This collection of studies helps to reinforce Jacobs's views about the importance of diverse human activity and visual interest, but with the additional observation that a sense of mystery, and green space or trees, make a street more attractive, and walkable. More walkable streets lead to more vibrant and cohesive neighbourhoods, as everyone from the schoolchild to the pensioner treads the tarmac.

## Traffic noise

Traffic is one of the twenty-first century's most challenging problems, and has a profound effect on our well-being. Donald Appleyard, Professor of Urban Design at the University of California, compared life on 'heavy, medium, and light' traffic streets. Examining the street with heavy traffic, he found that people had abandoned it altogether, leaving it to the buses, lorries and cars. In contrast, residents spent more time on the street with light traffic – ambling or shopping, drinking a latte or a glass of wine. Crucially, they also looked out for each other more and protected the area. There was a greater feeling of ownership and defended territory. (These findings were replicated in Bristol, UK in 2011, so they are still relevant in the twenty-first century.) As Jacobs would have predicted, this increased sense of ownership made people living on those streets much happier. Appleyard underlined the contrast in social capital caused by light and heavy traffic: 'On the one hand alienation, on the other friendliness and involvement.' Quieter streets were, he concluded, more livable.

Noise from traffic, railways or industry can harm a community, but it can adversely affect our mental and physical health if it also invades the buildings we inhabit. As well as making us tense and irritable, it can affect our decision-making, working memory and the regulation of emotions – collectively known as executive functioning (EF). As a city grows, so too does the danger of noise pollution, and this in turn becomes an important public health issue. This underlines why city planners must think about zoning – but we will return to this subject after looking at a few studies that considered the effects of noise in different neighbourhood settings.

In one study of schoolchildren, the EF of boys decreased in proportion to the amount of road-traffic noise to which they were exposed. Interestingly, the same relationship has not been consistently demonstrated in girls, who are thought to be less susceptible in general to problems with attention.

This RANCH project (Road Traffic and Aircraft Noise Exposure and Children's Cognition and Health) was the first study to examine the effect of exposure to aircraft and road traffic on reading comprehension in children. It was a large study, conducted in over 2,000 children, aged 9–10 years, who were being educated in 89 schools around three major hub airports: Amsterdam Schiphol, Madrid Barajas, and London Heathrow. High levels of aircraft noise impaired children's reading comprehension and recognition memory in all three countries. The traffic noise was not particularly high in this study, but when it was present it increased the effect of aircraft noise and multiplied the annoyance of the children. Another study found that learning in children is adversely affected by both traffic and aircraft noise, with evidence that it creates problems with sustaining attention and memory and also compromises reading comprehension. It is possible that intermittent noise is worse than continuous noise in its cognitive effects.

A detrimental effect of noise is not seen just in children, though. Adults experience ill effects too. Disturbed sleep is a major issue, which leads to low energy levels and poor concentration. Daytime noise is also intensely annoying and stressful, and it stops people from relaxing. It affects your willingness to socialise. In the longer term, it leads to anxiety disorders and depression. The combination of noise from more than one source (construction noise and traffic noise) is more disruptive of sleep than either source alone.

Can we adapt to noise pollution created by traffic? Neil Weinstein of Rutgers, The State University of New Jersey, set out to study this very question using a follow-up design. He was able to interview residents before and after a major new highway was constructed beside their homes – four months and then sixteen months after it opened. It linked up other highways with high levels of traffic, so the amount of traffic noise created was significant.

The highway passed through a fully developed suburban community that consisted almost entirely of single family houses. Some houses had been demolished to make room for it. All the homes that were selected for the study were expected to be within a '70 decibel contour' of noise pollution, as calculated by a pre-construction noise impact study.

Weinstein measured three ways the noise might affect people:

1. Behaviour (hampering various activities like listening to the TV or radio, disturbing sleep or harming health)
2. Annoyance about the negative effects
3. Preoccupation with the noise (noise focus)

In the event, scores on all three were highly correlated, so they were combined to give a total disturbance score. Weinstein came up with three main findings:

1. Self-reported noise disturbance was quite stable over time

2.  There was no significant adaptation to the noise over the one-year interval.
3.  Respondents became more pessimistic about their ability to adapt to the noise as time went by.

Since Weinstein's study some thirty years ago we now accept that noise disturbance is a major public health issue, and annoyance is the biggest predictor of ill health. This can be affected by personality and the meaning of the noise, but ultimately it is the loudness of the noise that has the biggest impact on annoyance. Insomnia caused by noise can be manifest in difficulty getting off to sleep, waking in the middle of the night, or early morning wakening. Noise also makes the stages of sleep shallower, making sleep less refreshing. Intermittent noise – like aircraft flying over, or buses passing – is more disturbing than continuous traffic noise. It is not just noise at night which affects sleep. Noise experienced only in the day can disturb the quality of sleep later, because of the accumulation of stress.

Adaptation to traffic noise is reported by some people, who state that their sleep improves as they 'get used to' noise, but measures of brain electrical activity (using the electroencephalograph) show no real improvements in the amount or quality of sleep: there is a paucity of deep sleep compared with rapid eye movement (REM) sleep. Noise makes us aroused and triggers a physiological stress response – including higher levels of adrenaline. Over time this can have adverse health outcomes. Long-term exposure to traffic noise in adults is associated with hypertension (raised blood pressure), irrespective of age.

The feeling that you have some control over when you are exposed to noise (that you can escape from it) can reduce its impact: physiological measures of stress (like blood pressure and skin conductance) and cognitive functions (like concentration and working memory) are less affected. On the other hand, if noise can be avoided for periods of time, the adverse effects are multiplied when the level of noise exceeds what is expected. In other words, intermittent and unexpectedly loud noise has more adverse effects than continuous noise, and the effects can persist for years.

If we are able to avoid noise by spending more time in the quieter parts of our homes (not facing a busy street), this could protect us from noise-related stress. A study in Sweden looked at this very question. It is reported that in Sweden nearly one million adults, or 22 per cent of the Swedish population, are disturbed by noise in their homes. In residential areas, road traffic is normally the dominant noise source. Evy Öhrström and colleagues at the Department of Environmental Medicine, Gothenburg University, conducted a study of 956 individuals aged 18–75 years.

They compared homes that were exposed to a noise level of 45–68 decibels on all sides with homes that had a quieter side (10–20 decibels quieter). They found clear evidence of the health benefits of having access to quiet, noise-shielded indoor and outdoor sections. Noise adversely affected sleep, energy, stress, anger, irritability, general annoyance levels, the ability to relax and the ability to socialise – and levels were all significantly improved if there was access to a quieter side of the home. The effects were particularly dramatic when noise levels on the worst side were above 60 decibels. When noise levels were below 45 decibels on either side, there were no significant psychological health problems.

It is interesting to consider whether the relatively low density of cities in Sweden, and perhaps a greater reliance on the car, might be a factor in the high prevalence of noise disturbance in the country. The reason for this assertion, is that, counter-intuitively, people in denser cities tend to use up less energy getting around. This implies that there is less traffic, perhaps because cars are impractical, and because people walk or take public transport, much of which might be underground.

We are also exposed to a lot of noise from other human beings in the city. However, the human voice appears to be much less stressful than traffic noise. In fact, sometimes the noise of humans is welcome, if we identify with the group making the noise. Research conducted in northern India found that the distress caused by the 'loud, continuous and cacophonous noise' produced during the Mela, a religious festival, depended on the perceived source of the noise.

The same noise was experienced more positively (and listened to longer) when attributed to the festival rather than to a non-festival source. Also, for those participating in the Mela, noises judged as having a religious quality were reported as more positive than noises that were not. A key moderating factor in determining a positive evaluation of the noise was the participants' social identity as a pilgrim. So, annoyance arising from the human voice will depend on whether you determine that the context is acceptable. Being woken in your city apartment by some drunken youths shouting expletives might make you seethe with anger. By contrast, hearing carols sung at Christmas time might be intrusive, but the emotional reaction will be different.

In general a gentle hubbub is quite soothing, especially for children. In fact, studies have demonstrated that children sleep better with the background noise of human voices than they do in an atmosphere of total silence. The presence of adult voices signals protection and security.

## Air pollution

Where you find traffic, you will usually find air pollution, which also has effects on your mental health. The top five most polluted cities in the world are all in California: Bakersfield, Hanford, Los Angeles, Visalia and Fresno. With the exception of San Francisco and a few coastal towns, California is a state in love with the car. Its towns and cities are designed with virtually no public transport: they sprawl. Walking and cycling from one neighbourhood to another, or from home to a basic amenity like a hospital, is largely impossible. Other highly polluted cities include New Mexico and New York City, where tower blocks form a barrier to the dissipation of air-based toxins.

Most research on the effects of urban air pollution has focused on particulates – tiny soot particles spewed from traffic, factories and power plants. Although the main interest has been the adverse effects of particulates on the cardiovascular system, attention is now being paid to psychological effects. It is becoming clear that air pollution affects the brain. A study in New York City followed children from before birth to age six or seven. It found that a child's exposure in the womb to polycyclic aromatic hydrocarbons (a product of burning fossil fuels) was associated with more attention problems, anxiety and depression in their later development. Portuguese re-searchers explored the relationship between psychological health and living in industrial areas. They found that people who lived in areas associated with greater levels of air pollution scored higher on tests of anxiety and depression. In Michigan, students at public schools who lived in polluted industrial areas had lower attendance rates and higher rates of exam failure than non-polluted public schools. Socio-economic status was the same for both.

Animal studies give a clue about what might be happening in the human brain as a result of pollution. The brains of dogs living in polluted areas of Mexico City had more neurofibrillary tangles and amyloid in their brains than dogs in non-polluted areas. These are inflammatory markers associated with Alzheimer's Disease. A study of the effects of exposure to soot in mice demonstrated that they took longer to learn a maze puzzle, and had more 'depressive' behaviours, reversed by mouse-sized doses of antidepressants. Their brains had higher levels of cytokines, a marker of inflammation, and fewer connections between brain cells concerned with spatial memory in the hippocampus.

## Unhealthy behaviour

Jasmin Honold at the Humboldt University of Berlin was interested in the effect of three environmental burdens – traffic noise, air pollution and lack of green space – on health behaviour.

She and her fellow researchers compared neighbourhood blocks in Berlin's inner city with high levels and low levels of these burdens. All blocks had the same architecture and were in close proximity to each other (roughly 600–700 metres apart). The high-burden blocks had street noise levels above 65 decibels day and night. Sources of noise included road traffic, trams, above-ground metros and railways. They had less than 0.1 square metres of public green space per resident within a 500-metre radius (compared with 6 square metres in the low-burden blocks). They also had high peak levels of particulates and nitrous oxide at many times in the year. Residents from the low-burden blocks had more apartments with a balcony, terrace, patio or shared garden and more apartments without windows facing the street.

The researchers sent out 2,000 surveys, of which 428 were returned. Residents from high-burden blocks felt more impaired, annoyed or threatened by traffic noise and air pollution compared to residents from low-burden blocks. Given what we have learnt so far about noise annoyance leading to health problems, and the restorative effect of green space, we would predict poorer physical and mental health in the high-burden blocks. However, the researchers were surprised to discover that residents from high-burden blocks did *not* report more psychological symptoms, or more stress-related physical symptoms. What the authors did uncover, though, was a potential health time bomb: the residents in the high-burden blocks had less healthy lifestyles – they smoked more, less exercise and drank marginally more alcohol. After accounting for gender, education level and employment status, these differences still held true.

This was an important finding, because such unhealthy lifestyles are normally attributed to having a lower social status, but the social status of residents in low- and high-burden blocks was roughly comparable. These results are consistent with other research that has shown an increase in the rate of smoking when people are exposed to more noise. The lack of green space deprives the residents of a healthier antidote to stress – exercise.

Research like this is important, because it suggests that simple changes to the environment should, in the long run, improve the health of people living in high-burden city apartments. They do not need to cost much. For example, a strip of roadside vegetation, including trees and shrubs, can improve the amount of green space while also reducing air and noise pollution. Unused brownfield sites can be converted to parks, like in the successful development of Brooklyn's Riverside Park. The researchers also suggest, 'If public green spaces cannot be added in areas that lack [it], it should be compensated by other measures to involve residents in regular physical exercise. This might be achieved by providing more gyms, sport halls or sport programs, and by supporting sport unions.'

## A walkshed life

A common-sense approach to reducing traffic noise and carbon emissions is to design (or redesign) our cities in such a way that we don't feel the need to travel by car so much. This is not just about providing better public transport, but about encouraging localism. We can do this in a number of ways. We can make sure that most things we need are within walking distance. Where space is tight, this can be done by taking advantage of unused spaces.

Cities are stockpiles of unused capacities. Pop-up spaces make good use of vacant spaces and, by increasing the available facilities, tempt us to stay in our own local community.

Travelling around is also reduced when a public building takes on many functions. The multistorey car park in Miami is a famous example (see overleaf). It is used for running, a yoga class, a function hall and even a place to get married. There is simply no need to travel when everything is in one place.

The many functions of a Miami multistorey car park

Research shows that people give up their cars altogether if they are surrounded by places that make them feel at home. City dwellers are increasingly looking for a 'walkshed life' – a town-planning term that has become part of the general lexicon. The walkshed refers to the area of a neighbourhood that is contained within a reasonable walking distance of where you live. The radius of the circle containing this territory could be defined in distance or in time – half a mile, or a ten-minute walk. In the ideal walkshed life, all things that you needed would be within this ten-minute walk. This dream neighbourhood could be completely car-free.

Another way of reducing traffic is to use zoning to encourage the use of public transport. Intelligent urban planning can restrict new residential developments to zones that are within a ten-minute walk of a tram or subway. A good example of this is the zoning strategy in New York City.

As an aside, the elderly benefit from neighbourhoods where they can walk to see their friends. Visiting behaviour was compared in San Francisco and San Antonio. In San Francisco, homes are smaller and closer together, and there are more convenience stores within walking distance. In San Antonio, there is more space. Homes are more spread out, and there are fewer local shops: larger, more remote shopping centres are provided instead, which need to be reached by car. Social visiting among the old was twice as high in San Francisco than in San Antonio: 61% visited friends at least once per week, compared with 35% in San Antonio. In San Antonio, 42% of residents *never* visited their friends, compared to 14% in San Francisco.

Interestingly, in the more close-knit communities of San Francisco, there were more long trips made to public leisure places than in other cities. It seems that more local social behaviour leads to more engagement in the wider social fabric of a city. The implications are clear: in order to maximise prosocial behaviour among the elderly, give them a walkshed life.

In summary, a walkshed life can combat the problems inherent in moving large numbers of people around, and the psychological problems that go with it. There might also be social benefits, as we have seen in the study on the elderly. We should be able to walk to the main street, which provides a vital hub for social contact. It is at the heart of the neighbourhood. The most vibrant main streets have a variety of small businesses, and affordable rents. In dense cities, where homes might be smaller, the street becomes the place to meet friends. In fact, where housing is of higher density, street life is more vibrant – streets are owned by the community and they become social spaces.

Streets in general contribute to a pleasant local neighbourhood if they are clean and visually complex, but on a human scale. We need to pay attention to aspects that make streets more appealing and walkable, including the planting of trees and the strips between road and pavement. Both residential and main streets should not be dominated by traffic, which pushes people away. Traffic noise causes both mental and physical health problems, through direct stress, the effects of air pollution, and by encouraging unhealthy behaviours like smoking. Another important consideration, though, is safety. Security is the second priority of the home after shelter, but the need to feel safe extends beyond those four walls into the wider neighbourhood.

Chapter 10

# Protecting the territory

We should feel safe on our streets, and in the bits of public space around them. Our homes, and the private gardens around them, are territories to be defended – but the more we feel connected to the local neighbourhood, the more this feels like an extension of our territory, and the more we want to defend it too.

Positive communities look after each other because they have built social capital (community ties marked by reciprocity, trust and cooperation) over years. This is closely related to a feeling of ownership and identity – a sense of place. If we feel that we have a stake in a neighbourhood, and it has a stake in us, we will look after its appearance. This is important. A neighbourhood that looks neglected attracts crime.

There is another major physical factor that affects crime, and this is more to do with design. Are the spaces around our homes easy to see into from the home or the street? If spaces can be seen, they are less likely to harbour criminals. Peering eyes are the most effective deterrent against unwanted trespassers. Even if we do not have a clear view, it is preferable that our neighbours across the road do, or people in passing cars. In other words, our homes should be surrounded by what environmental psychologists call *defensible space.* The man behind this concept was the consulting architect Oscar Newman.

In New York state, a study of 100 housing projects revealed that crime was generally higher (per capita) in large buildings, but the most important factor was related to the public spaces, such as yards, lifts, lobbies, alleyways, subways and stairwells. What mattered was how hidden they were from the views of surrounding homes and how difficult they were to navigate and escape from in a hurry. These were the incubators of crime. The research conclusions were obvious – a neighbourhood should have open space that is easily guarded and protected. More specifically, they spelled out four rules for architects and town planners to consider when designing a housing development:

1. Don't just provide communal open space. Provide personal areas of territory (like gardens, yards and balconies), which people will be more likely to protect because they take ownership of them
2. Avoid spaces that cannot easily be seen by residents.
3. Make sure a block has the appearance of being secure and well maintained – this 'secure image' deters intruders
4. Provide safe and easy access to the surrounding area – street vistas, and roads, that also provide adequate surveillance

It is all very well to lay out some rules for good housing blocks, but what about the ones that are already blighted by poorly defended spaces? Can anything be done to improve them? The answer is – it depends.

## The Diggs Town project

A good example of a blighted neighbourhood that was turned around by improving its security is the Diggs Town Project in Norfolk, Virginia, USA. This was a low-rise public housing project mainly populated by single African-American women and their children, and in the 1980s it was plagued by unemployment, crime, drugs and decay. Residents had lost control of the streets and began to fear for their lives.

The problem was not the demographic (other housing projects with a similar demographic did not suffer the same problems); the problem was the street pattern. The inner parts of the project were completely inaccessible by road, preventing any through traffic, including police patrol cars. Isolated from the eyes of passing drivers and passengers, the centre became a hub of criminal activity. In other words, the centre became one large *indefensible space.* Connected with this was the problem of lack of ownership of outside space – all green open space was considered public. This meant that no one took ownership; it became neglected, and quickly deteriorated into dangerous territory – used at will by gangs. In addition, without streets, pavements or fenced-off front lawns, anyone could wander up to a building and look in the windows.

In 1990 the Norfolk Redevelopment and Housing Authority awarded Urban Design Associates $17 million to redevelop Diggs Town. With the help of social psychologists they diagnosed the problem and then realised that the solution was simple: the people needed streets. Pedestrian walkways were replaced by roads, and parking islands were provided.

As well as improving the general surveillance of the estate, the streets also allowed for private allocation of fenced-off open space, thereby deterring gangs from wandering freely.

According to a community police officer, police calls dropped from 25–30 per day to 2–3 per week. Not only did the crime rate fall, but the residents started to take ownership of their territory again. After only a matter of months the community seemed to have achieved a renewed sense of pride. This is a striking example of how improvements in urban design can improve the safety of a neighbourhood.

## Robin Hood Gardens

About ten years ago, Robin Hood Gardens in east London, a very British version of concrete high-rise living (see opposite) was being considered for demolition by the local council, such was the level of deterioration in the neighbourhood. The project was famous for its suspended concrete decks, the 'streets in the sky' (a phrase coined by the project's celebrated architects, the Smithsons). The intention of the decks was to foster a sense of community, because all the flats opened on to them, like a street. However, local residents complained of crime and vandalism, and of being hit by missiles when walking along the decks.

Robin Hood Gardens, Poplar, London

Almost as soon as the possibility of demolition was announced, a number of eminent architects called for English Heritage to protect Robin Hood Gardens from demolition on the grounds of architectural importance. These included Richard Rogers, designer of the Lloyd's Building, Pompidou Centre and Millennium Dome. Lord Rogers argued that 'Robin Hood Gardens has been appallingly neglected and, from the beginning, had been used as a sink estate to house those least capable of looking after themselves – much less their environment.' In other words, because of the choices made by the local council it had never stood a chance. This wasn't the fault of the building – it was the fault of the tenants and poor maintenance. It followed that if the building were refurbished, populated by a variety of tenants, and properly maintained, it could still provide good-quality homes for the future.

English Heritage were not convinced. The response of Margaret Hodge, Minister for Culture at the time, could be summarised with the retort, 'Well, you try living in it!' They refused to list it. No amount of refurbishment, they argued, would overcome its major design limitations. It had failed on a human level to provide a sense of security and community. The problems they listed included:

1. Indefensibly narrow, twisting stairwells. There are far too few of them and their tightness is uncomfortable and quite threatening. They have never provided adequate access to those long decks and people's front doors.
2. The decks themselves – perhaps because they are not particularly generous and overlook constant traffic – never did fulfil their brief to work as community-fostering 'streets in the sky'.
3. Tall boundary walls, intended to baffle traffic noise, feel like prison walls.
4. Bleak and dark entrance lobbies, with glass bricks instead of windows.
5. Isolated parking areas, where 'no-one can see what's happening and there's no easy way out.'

Demolition finally began in 2013, after years of wrangling. The project had begun with high ideals – to provide good-quality social housing for the poor – but had failed largely because of its dreary and limited communal spaces and indefensible concrete bunkers. It had also failed for the same reason that Diggs Town had failed: as well as having too many indefensible spaces, it had been cut off from its surroundings. Right from the beginning, the plan to locate the project in the middle of a ring of busy roads meant that it was isolated. There was no through traffic to supervise the communal land, or street life to enrich it.

## Centre Village

Unfortunately mistakes like these are still being made. In January 2016 the *Guardian* newspaper ran a feature on a social housing project in Winnipeg, Canada. Designed by the award-winning architects 5468796 Architecture, Centre Village was a huddle of white stucco buildings surrounding what was intended to be a serene, community-fostering central courtyard. With its bold, orange-framed windows, it was far from the generic image of social housing.

Architects Raja Moussaoui and Andrea Lacalamita visited the development, hoping to discover a successful model of social rejuvenation and community building. What they discovered were permanently closed blinds on the windows facing the courtyard. To their dismay this had become a 'magnet for drinking and drug-taking at all hours', with litter scattered across the ground. It was blighted by crime. The cooperative who had set up the venture had now abandoned the whole project, and put it up for sale to private developers.

How did it all go so wrong? The architects believed that the courtyard space was crucial for fostering a sense of community. Unfortunately, it was fatally flawed. Built to protect the residents from the cold winds of the long winters, it had no sightlines running through it from the street and surrounding areas. Thus it became the ideal hideout for addicts. Once again, a project with worthy intentions had become blighted by indefensible space.

It is not just the town planner that should learn from these examples. We, the *potential residents* of any housing estate, should also take heed. Ideally, before moving to any neighbourhood we should carefully survey it to check that it conforms to the four rules arising from the New York study. Are the homes well maintained? Is there a sense of ownership of the buildings and spaces around them? Are there no dark, hidden spaces? And is there a connection to the wider community through lively streets?

### Territorial markers

Building on the results of the New York study, researchers have compared the features of burgled houses with non-burgled houses in the same block. Non-burgled homes had salient features which communicated both privacy and individuality. These 'territorial markers' included: flags in windows, window boxes, well-tended front gardens, garden furniture, pruned hedges and picket fences. Territorial markers can be divided into primary and secondary. Primary markers are about defining private territory. Secondary markers indicate care and individuality; they are the personal touches. Both markers deter crime, but the secondary markers are even more powerful than the primary ones.

By contrast, the houses that were the most likely to be burgled looked less private and gave the appearance of being unoccupied and neglected. In addition, non-burgled homes had greater visual contact with neighbouring houses, confirming what other studies have concluded about the need for defensible space.

So far, we have considered a number of environmental conditions that are necessary to create a buzzing, safe, walkable neighbourhood, but we have not yet touched on the physical and social forces that actually bring people together. We will revisit the importance of identity and ownership later. Let us first consider successful examples of housing projects that have helped foster casual contact through good design. The best examples achieve the right balance between privacy and community.

# Chapter 11

# The spirit of place

Defining a sense of place was the preoccupation of Dr Per Gustafson of the Department of Sociology, Gothenburg University in Sweden. After conducting a painstaking series of interviews he was able to identify three common things that made people attached to local public places.

Spaces with a sense of place were distinctive, had a sense of continuity over time, and were valued. In other words, they had identity. However, a place also included the potential to change – to adapt to the changing needs of individuals or groups of people.

Distinctiveness is not just an objective judgment, it reflects the use of the space by a particular group or subculture. At the same time, a place is often distinctive based on its type – what it is used for, such as a café or meeting hall. In some ways, the categorisation makes it distinct in the neighbourhood but it also fits into a category with other similar places – it is both unique and not unique at the same time. The continuity of the place is similar to the feeling of permanence in the home. According to Gustafson, a meaningful place is 'connected to the life path of the individual through origin, length of residence, important events or life stages, or frequent visits'. Continuity is also inherent in a place if it has some historic value, or conjures up local traditions. Value is self-explanatory – a place is never indifferent. Without a value judgment, a space is meaningless.

The concept of change at first seems contradictory, but if the change has come about over a long period of time, due to the efforts of the local community, the sense of continuity is not necessarily disturbed. As Gustafson put it, people 'try to make places "their own" by forging social relations (e.g. visiting neighbours), by acquiring knowledge about the place, or by physically shaping the place. In these cases, places could be described in terms of personal projects; places may indeed even become collective projects, through people's participation in local social movements.'

A place that is cherished can be iconic and wrapped in a rich culture and mythology – like the stone circle of Stonehenge. In a cityscape our *genius loci* might be more prosaic, like an urban park or an urbane art deco coffee shop. A cherished space might even appear to be neglected to some but have a deep meaning to others – like the arches under Waterloo Station which play host to graffiti artists and fringe performing arts. Places represent the invisible weaving of culture (memories, beliefs, artistic symbols and histories), physicality (views, designs, natural phenomena and monuments) and people (the lived experience we have had there, with loved ones and other kindred spirits).

The Romantics hoped to 're-enchant' the land by art, but the truth is that the spirit of place can take time to evolve. There is a limit to what designers can achieve on their own in order to create a sense of place. If we, the end users, don't get involved in the planning right from the start, we will tend to disown whatever is designed, with the best of intentions, to revive our community.

## Disney housing

Perhaps the most spectacular example of this was built outside Paris in the early 1980s by Barcelona architect Ricardo Bofill, considered by some to be the Messiah of social housing. The projects were so ambitious in both magnitude and design that they became a place of pilgrimage for fashion photographers. Superficially, these buildings avoided the monotony of most social housing projects, embracing variation, decorative façades and big public spaces in between.

Ricardo Boffill's Arcades du Lac, near Paris

A famous example is the Arcades du Lac (see above), reviving classical porticos and architraves on an impressive scale – and regarded at the time as a veritable palace for the poor. Another example is Les Arènes de Picasso (see overleaf), made up of two giant drums, like Swiss cheeses, with rose windows and grand, Gaudí-inspired buttresses.

Around these buildings, Bofill built a series of avenues and squares, to recreate the image of a city, like a stage set. He wanted to remove the 'fractured nature of an unplanned city' in an attempt to avoid creating ghettos.

Ricardo Boffill's Les Arènes de Picasso, near Paris

But these buildings were criticised for being kitsch and narcissistic – they demand to be the centre of attention but ultimately they are superficial. They assert a particular identity, but there is no dialogue with the people who live there, so the identity lacks depth. Their overwhelming scale has proved oppressive, and the places between the monumental towers were always uninviting. The faux piazzas lacked meaning to the people using them. Spaces between buildings that are on a human scale are much more meaningful: they encourage planting in front of homes and coincidental meetings with neighbours. They create a sense of ownership. Although the drama of Bofill's creations avoided the monotony of the worst of the Paris high-rise projects, the whole development only really succeeded as a backdrop for film-makers. It failed to enrich people's lives. Film sets do not make livable homes.

Projects like this will never be about real community. If a variety of architectural styles is imposed on a housing project, this will never map on to an authentic sense of the diversity of the people in that neighbourhood. The project will reflect the architect's idea of place, not ours. Even if an architect's dream appears to meet some of our needs perfectly, any sense of community will struggle to develop if we, the residents, are not involved in the process. Place is essentially about a sense of ownership – without this, what is left is a space.

In the late 1990s, the Sunnyside neighbourhood in Portland, Oregon, USA, was dilapidated and plagued by problems of alienation, littering, crime and increased rates of psychological problems. In an attempt to invigorate 'neighbourhood stewardship', the community organised and created a public gathering space called the Sunnyside Plaza. Together they painted a giant sunflower in the middle of an intersection and installed several interactive art features. According to an academic report, the social capital increased as a result of this 'collective place-making', thus revitalising the community and stimulating a sense of well-being through increased social contacts.

The contribution of local users in the design process in renovating or customising a community adds real meaning and hence a sense of place. This requires architects to act unselfishly by giving up a significant amount of authorship in a design. In essence, it is architecture without ego.

Such developments have been seen to work very well. Community architecture projects can work at their best when tenant activists become the architects. Charlie

Baker is one such example. A photo-journalist living in a run-down neighbourhood in Hulme, Manchester, he was forthright in his commitment to renovating the area.

He decided that the best way to effect change was to train as an architect. After he completed his training, he founded Build for Change, a community-based cooperative that renovated the community's homes and public facilities with the intense input of its residents. *Hulme Ten Years On*, a local government publication, cites user participation as a key factor in the 'improved quality of life' of its residents. Baker's next project, in London Fields in Hackney, northeast London brought together the council and squatters of a disused block of offices to agree to a new live-work scheme. He called this process the Community Gateway Model for turning an area around. It has now become a standard approach for renovating deprived urban areas.

## Facebook architecture

The rise of social media has provided new opportunities for community involvement in the design of new public buildings. When a much-loved leisure centre in the seaside resort of Fire Island Pines, New York State, burnt down, the owners employed a radical group of architects to build a replacement. The company Architizer, led by architect Marc Kushner, prides itself on its use of social media to foster community involvement and receive valuable feedback on its proposed designs. Kushner's proposed replacement was somewhat radical and bold (see opposite), and both he and his client were worried that the local residents might not be ready for their radically different design.

Fire Island Pines Pavilion, New York

Public consultations at the planning stage provide useful feedback on the first draft of a new design. They are an important part of the design process, but forums in local authority buildings are often poorly attended; they can be dominated by those who shout the loudest, and who do not speak for the whole community. For these forward-thinking architects, harnessing the speed and reach of the Internet was a no-brainer. They put photorealistic renderings of their proposed building on Facebook and Instagram two years before it was due to be built. Within days these images were shared, reposted and commented on by thousands of people who might never have stepped into a council building.

When the comments were almost entirely positive, the architects knew that they had got the design right. When the building was finally constructed, it looked almost exactly like the renderings that had met with approval online, so there were no nasty surprises for the community. As the lead architect Marc Kushner put it, 'The building was already part of the community.'

Then, during the first summer after opening, the building hit the social media again, except that this time the images being circulated were photos taken by visitors on their smartphones. Not only was the community owning these images, but people were demonstrating how the building was being used in the real world – how they interacted in positive ways with it. This is the best feedback an architect could have. Collectively, these real, personal narratives imbued the building with a sense of place, reaching across the real and virtual worlds. According to Kushner, 'The building had become media.'

The viral speed of Facebook and Google can now inform the future of design in a way that was never possible before. Architects can reach out to the public and receive rapid and democratic responses. And they are freer in their feedback on the Internet; they become less intimidated by architecture. From beginning to end, the Internet helps architects to learn – and the feedback from one project will inform the next. If you liked that, would you like this? You didn't like this as much, so what if we did this?

With the advent of social media we now have the opportunity to create and own our own public spaces like never before. As Kushner reminds us, the history of architecture in the twentieth century was about the imposition of buildings on people – whether they were brutalist concrete buildings, with their non-human scale and tiny windows, or bad pastiches of what a library or gallery or some other public building should look like. Since the growth of the Internet, bad buildings can no longer escape negative feedback and post-mortems. The Internet does not hold back in its vitriol when buildings are imposed, out of context, ignoring their surroundings and their users. Social media has connected us with architecture, and we can be an essential part of the design process. Architects who ignore social media are missing an important step, because once the building is constructed, it is too late to correct mistakes, and the Internet will be unforgiving.

Another Internet-fueled development – crowd-sourcing – means that there may be no single client for the architect any more. The online community can get behind an architect's dream and help to fund it – like the proposed swimming platform in the East River of New York. Crowd sourcing raised half a million dollars for this project.

Kushner has commented, 'Architects already know how to make buildings that are greener, smarter, friendlier, we were just waiting for you to want them.' There is an inherent contradiction here. The statement implies that the Internet is just a new method for architects to impose their visions. In fact, the Internet provides a dialogue between architects and people before the first brick is laid. It informs designers about the specific human needs in a community. Many architects have the problem-solving skills and imagination to rejuvenate communities, but they can make mistakes. The way that their plans are implemented can and should be dictated by us, through the power of new media.

## Community versus big business

When corporations try to ape a community's independent character for commercial ends, the community often reasserts itself. In the lead-up to London's 2012 Olympics, the residents of nearby Hackney Wick, a once affordable former industrial location where artists had made their homes, was fast becoming gentrified. The Coca-Cola

Olympic mural, painted without consultation on the side of a disused warehouse, became a symbol of the fast-disappearing artistic community, priced out by speculators. The offending mural was quickly defaced with the word 'shame'. In response, the mural was painted over with grey paint, except for the huge red initials 'HW'. The adapted mural stridently reasserted the unique character of Hackney Wick's diverse artistic community.

Clearly, artistic communities help to give an urban centre a sense of place. In Hackney they transformed faceless warehouses into live-work units for artists. Cafés and bars then sprang up to serve the community. The result was an authentic and inspirational hub, uncontaminated by big business and estate-agent spin. Other bright young urbanites then moved in. They rejected the already gentrified London high streets, complete with their chain coffee bars and estate agents, in favour of independently run places with a sense of ownership and community. Of course, in so doing, the buzz of the hipster influx destroys the original reason for the draw, and the sense of place quickly disappears. All that is left is something that apes what was once authentic.


## A sense of history

The more distinctive a place, by virtue of its local history, the more likely the local community will become attached to it. For example, Dr Maria Lewicka, of the University of Warsaw, has argued that having the opportunity to *rediscover* an area's local history, after major political change, might have a powerful effect on our attachment to it. Rediscovering place has been extremely important in Poland in recent years. After the Second World War, Poland's territory was redrawn by the Allies, leading to a vast movement of people into Poland from what are now the Baltic states and from Germany. Soviet Communism was a repressive experience for the average Pole, and for many people that life is within living memory.

Until 1989 media celebration of local cultural roots, religious or otherwise, was banned by the Soviets. Once censorship was removed there was, predictably, a volcanic eruption of publications and public discussions concerning family roots, family histories, and memories of places associated with these histories, past and present. At the same time, decentralisation of government was encouraging more localism.

In an attempt to explore the impact of history on attachment, Dr Lewicka examined data from the Polish Public Opinion Research Center – a sample of 1,328 citizens from three different Polish regions, with different geographical histories. Place attachment and neighbourhood ties were significantly lower in the less conservative, newly acquired western and northern territories than in the eastern territories and in Galicia (formerly part of Austria, in the south). The implication was that rediscovering our roots can have a direct effect on our civic pride and civic activity, prompting Polish authorities to insist that study of local history should be built into every school curriculum.

Related to Lewicka's research is the work of Jeremy Wells and Elizabeth Baldwin of Roger Williams University, Bristol, Rhode Island and Clemson University, South Carolina. They compared the attitudes of residents towards a new urbanist development called L'On in Mount Pleasant, and a historic district in Charleston, both in South Carolina. These were good places for comparison because both had a similar population density, layout and design, but of very different vintages. The essential difference between the two towns was as predicted: the historic neighbourhood instilled 'creative fantasies in the minds of the informants based on a hypothetical past of their own creation'. This age value had a direct and strong effect on the residents' emotional attachment to the more historic neighbourhood. However, to their surprise, the features of these two towns that evoked the strongest sense of attachment tended to be natural features of the landscape, 'such as gates, fountains, trees, and gardens rather than buildings'. Residents valued the mystery that these natural elements created – vistas and buildings gradually revealed themselves when walking along.

Arguably, this research on *placeness* in towns cannot be directly applied to the city. Dr Hernan Casakin of Ariel University in Israel was interested in the effect of the size of a city on sense of identity in the local neighbourhood and the wider city. More than 200 Israelis were studied, with 23% of participants living in large cities (of more than 500,000 inhabitants), 54% in medium-sized cities (of 20,000–500,000 inhabitants) and the remaining 27% in small settlements (of less than 20,000 inhabitants).

Place identity was greater in large cities compared to small and medium-sized cities. Identity tended to predict the amount of emotional attachment, although, intriguingly, this was not the case for the medium-sized cities. The explanation offered was that the large cities were big enough to have more facilities and better infrastructure, while small cities tended to be more close-knit. The medium-sized city missed out on both.

### What makes us get involved?
We have seen that in order to build a thriving neighbourhood community we need to be actively

involved in it – joining local groups, getting involved in regeneration, traffic calming, organising social and cultural events, and so on. But what influences the amount of civic activity we engage in? Some research has shown a link between how attached we are to a place and how much we contribute to it. This seems like common sense. But what kind of people become more attached to a place? And is attachment the only factor at play?

Some early research suggested that low-income groups become more attached to a local neighbourhood. However, if impoverished and marginalised social groups become 'localised' without necessarily desiring to be so, this does not equate to real attachment. On the other hand, there is some evidence to suggest that if we have a lot of attachment to a place this will inhibit our own economic and social progress – we will be less equipped to move where the work is, or to seek out new experiences. Or we might just lack the motivation to move away because of greater family ties. Perhaps different explanations apply for different groups of people, but the relative strength of these effects is not known.

Such explanations for local attachment are increasingly challenged by more sophisticated research. There is evidence to show that people's bonds with the places in which they live might be *increased* by their opportunity to move and travel. For example, people who lived in Radom, a satellite town of Warsaw, but who commuted to work in the city, felt a greater attachment to their home town than those who lived and worked in Radom. Perhaps the heart grows fonder, or perhaps the anonymity of the city reminds them how important it is to have some stable roots.

However, feeling attached to a community is not sufficient in itself to translate into action. In the city, it tends to be the more creative, better educated and entrepreneurial who get involved. If a neighbourhood attracts a lot of people with this creative potential, it is said to have a high level of cultural capital.

Dr Lewicka used data from the Polish Public Opinion Center to show that increased cultural capital translated into increased civic activity, but an interest in local historical roots was also important. High levels of poverty and hopelessness in an area tended to reduce both: deprivation caused a detachment from the past, reduced feelings of attachment, and decreased civic activity.

Civic activity in a neighborhood also relies on social capital – the number of ties you have to your neighbours. Lewicka used a process called structural equation modelling (SEM) to determine which of the two forms of capital was most predictive of civic involvement. She concluded that cultural capital was the strongest influence over community activity, emphasising the long tradition in Poland of the intelligentsia, the cultural elite, devoting their lives to public causes. However, this is a phenomenon found in most civilised nations. So, Dr Lewicka determined that an interest in cultural roots played the role of a true 'go-between', by being positively connected to both social and cultural capital. Consistent with this idea was evidence that cultural capital was attracted more to areas of Poland that were being rediscovered following the collapse of the Iron Curtain – where the population had been displaced during the war, as opposed to areas where there had been more historic continuity.

She confirmed that reports of feeling 'attached' to a place were not related to civic activity per se. You had to have evidence of strong ties and a keen interest in family and place history as well. So, if someone says they feel attachment to a place, you need to dig a bit deeper to see if this attachment has the potential to turn into action. An attachment could be merely ideological. As Lewicka puts it, 'It is not enough to be fond of a place – a locally based social network is necessary to help convert emotion into action.'

Another interesting finding was that there was no strong correlation between the amount of time spent in a place and the strength of neighbourhood ties. This could explain why people who commute or travel away more often are not necessarily less connected in the community. The amount of time spent there has little to do with it. Presumably it's about the quality of time, not the quantity. Also, and consistent with the study of Israeli cities, people who developed strong local ties also tended to feel more connected to places in the wider city.

### Building a community

The British architect Eric Lyons strongly believed that privacy was given too much importance in the modern world when compared to the need for the kind of casual social contact that builds a community. Of course, it was not always like this. The *petit bourgeois* preoccupation with privacy had barely existed in the West until the Victorian era.

Lyons argued that homes which insist on absolute privacy become a jail for their inhabitants. They are isolating. He pointed to the absurdity of the suburban detached home, with its illusion of exclusivity. He made medium-density urban housing for the city, which sometimes erred on the side of exposing people too much, but the best examples of his work achieved a workable compromise: the need to see out was in balance with the need for refuge. His designs allowed residents to hide away when they wanted. Choice is the key to successful housing – having the *option* for social contact built in to the housing design, but without obligation. We should be able to opt out of being a matey neighbour, but opt in to more gregarious activities when we want. We should not have to choose 'once and for all' if we want one or the other at the point of choosing a home.

The suburban family homes built from the 1940s onwards provide the illusion of total privacy – of no one living next door for miles, when in fact the neighbours are just a few feet away. This type of home offers no choice for opting in. If we are going to build houses next to each other in towns and cities, we might as well design them in groups, to give us the option of casual contact. In 1930s Germany, Bruno Taut in conjunction with the chief city planner devised a new breed of *Siedlungen* (housing estates). The distinct aim was to breed social interaction between residents. A fine example and one that later received UNESCO heritage-listing is the Hufeisensiedlung (Horseshoe Estate) in Neukölln, in south Berlin. The blocks of flats were a maximum of six storeys high and faced into a green courtyard containing a careful mixture of private space (near the buildings) and central communal space. The mini communities that they fostered provided enough individuality while still being social.

Some architects have gone a step further, providing large common areas for eating and working. However, it can be argued that the most successful examples of community building within the city are those that have been built or adapted by the occupants: communities like Christiania, Walters Way, Quinta Monroy and Fish

Island. And this leads us to the concepts of ownership and sense of place.

In the case of Walters Way, what was once social housing has become private, and many of the self-builders have moved on, but the strong sense of community lives on in cultural memory. Children play together in the street, residents collaborate on more eco-friendly ways of living. In 2015 some residents were interviewed for a short film for the Architecture Association. 'It doesn't feel like London,' one mother said. A male resident expanded further: 'The doors are open during the summer months, and the kids are just going in and out of the houses. Once a year we have a street party. Maybe three to four hundred people would be on the street. We'll have a stage at the bottom (of the street). We'll have live music, a bouncy castle, three barbecues on the go.' As for communal parenting, 'There's quite a lot of impromptu childcare.'

The community feel is partly down to the design of the street – its winding course, the shape of the houses, and their angled positions, poking out from many trees and shrubs. However, the community was set in motion because it was a self-build project. The original residents had a strong sense of ownership because of this, and a strong sense of interdependence that developed during the construction process. This social capital has lived on in cultural memory. After a community is established, the people who are attracted to live there tend to share the same ethos. This is how all sustainable and harmonious communities persist through the generations. Anyone who thinks that communities cannot survive in the city should see this development.

## Understanding the headspace of neighbourhood

Great neighbourhoods are built on social capital (neighbourhood ties), cultural capital (individuals with creative potential) a sense of ownership and an interest in local history.

The sense of owning a neighbourhood goes beyond the literal. It is a state of mind that gives it a sense of place. A sense of place can be created in any public space, as long as the local community is consulted. For buildings and spaces to become meaningful, we need to identify with them. Communities that have lost a sense of cohesion can recover it again through active participation in regeneration schemes. This leads us to realise that social housing projects and public spaces designed or renovated without the involvement of residents are doomed to almost inevitable failure.

Neighbourhoods are built on good design and planning. They need a main street at their heart, with a variety of businesses, lots of greenery, visual interest and walkable streets, not drowned out by heavy traffic. Increasingly, our streets are being taken over by high-rise blocks, a reaction to the growing populations of our cities. In the next chapter we will look at their effect on neighbourhoods and our general wellbeing.

# Part Four

# High-rise Living

All the evidence accumulated over several decades cast a critical light on the high-rise as a viable social structure, but cost-effectiveness . . . kept pushing these vertical townships into the sky.

*High-Rise*, J. G. Ballard

In Chapter 9, we looked at how the formidable activist Jane Jacobs fought the urban planning doctrine of the 1950s and 1960s, when swathes of dilapidated terraced housing, with its buzzing main streets, shops and cafés, were cleared to make way for tower blocks. These high-rise buildings promised better access to light and air, and great views. They were designed to be self-contained, vertical communities – both the planners and architects assumed that neighbours on each level would get to know each other. But have the high-rises lived up to their early promise? Have they preserved elements of neighbourhood that were evident in many of the streets they replaced?

Jacobs noticed that early examples seemed to kill life on the streets around them, but is this always the case? If high-rises have been successful in producing self-contained communities, does this matter? Can they even create a sense of place if well designed? Given the immense controversy surrounding the early experiments with high-rise living for the poor, and the huge proliferation of the mega-apartment block in recent decades, devoting several chapters to answering these questions is justified.

One in six European homes are located in high-rise blocks, and more and more are being built. In London the long protected views of St Paul's Cathedral are under threat and many worry that the city will soon become a 'Dubai-on-Thames'. Increasingly, executives choose to live in these new power blocks, while at the other end of the socio-economic scale, social housing is still being provided in high-rise buildings.

As high-rise living becomes more and more commonplace, it is increasingly important to know what effect living high in the sky has on our mental wellbeing. Should we choose to live high up if we have the choice? A penthouse might be an aspiration, but is it what we need to feel good, or just the opposite? The higher up we live in a city, the less the traffic noise and the better the view. If we are lucky enough to have panoramic views, these can be truly awe-inspiring and inspirational. They also meet our primeval need for prospect – surveying local and distant territories.

# Chapter 12

# Vertigo and other fears

It seems obvious, but it is not always acknowledged, that high-rises might trigger vertigo in people who are scared of heights. In March 2013 a judge made an unusual decision to order a London council to rehouse a tenant who was living in a high-rise block. After a long-running legal battle, the Court of Appeal ruled that Westminster Council must offer Mrs El-Dinnaoui and her family alternative accommodation.

The El-Dinnaoui family were living on the ninth floor, but required transfer to a larger property following the birth of their third child. They were offered a larger property in the same building, but seven floors higher up. After viewing this sixteenth-floor apartment, Mrs El-Dinnaoui collapsed in the lift and was taken to hospital. The subsequent medical report stated that she had had a panic attack, triggered by a 'lifelong fear of high buildings'. Following this traumatic incident Mr El-Dinnaoui refused the accommodation.

The council argued that Mrs El-Dinnaoui could 'learn to live' in the sixteenth-floor flat by covering the windows with camouflage, arguing that the ninth-floor flat was also high up; it just did not have as clear a view of the ground. This was not considered by the court to be an adequate response to Mrs El-Dinnaoui's mental health problems. Westminster Council were disappointed, to say the least, pointing out that 'Westminster is in the centre of the capital and inevitably much of our accommodation is in high-rise blocks.'

According to the environmental psychologist Robert Gifford, writing in *Architectural Science Review*, we are not designed to live high above the ground: 'Given the age of our species, living more than a few stories up is a very recent phenomenon. This tempts one to conclude that high rises are unnatural, and some would argue that what is unnatural must be, in some way, harmful.' He adds that high-rise residences 'evoke at least six fears' in the general population. These include a fear that a neighbour or loved one will fall or jump from a high window; a fear of being trapped in a fire; a fear of earthquake; a fear of a terrorist attack; a fear of strangers intruding into communal areas (and committing crime); and a fear of increased exposure to infectious diseases.

The fear of people jumping from a high-rise flat is something that has exercised the mind of Ann Haas, the director of the American Foundation for Suicide Prevention. In Manhattan, more than twenty per cent of suicide deaths are due to jumping off high buildings, whereas the national average is just two per cent. Haas explains, 'in an urban area like New York, there's access to lethal means every time you walk into a building.' An important determinant of suicide is ready access to lethal means. Death from jumping is certain, and it can be done on impulse, as a reaction to a negative life event.

In New York City, when suicide rates across all boroughs were compared, Manhattan, with its very high density of tall buildings, had a higher rate of suicide (per head), and the greater number of deaths by jumping added to the increase in this overall rate. A study in Singapore also suggested that the presence of tall buildings added to suicide statistics. The researchers compared suicide rates in 1960 to rates in 1976, during which time the percentage of the population who lived in high-rises had climbed from 9% to 51%. The overall suicide rate increased by 30% over this period. When examining trends in specific suicide methods, suicides by leaping had increased fourfold. In other words, leaping was not a substitution for another method; jumping from high-rises had disproportionately added to the suicide risk. That said, suicide remains a rare event.

Whether all six of Gifford's fears are rational and proportionate, or not, is unimportant. What is important is whether such fears have an impact on wellbeing over time. To determine that, we need to look at the research evidence. Not all residents of tower blocks will harbour one or more of Gifford's six fears. Even if they did at first, they might habituate. We are, after all, a remarkably adaptable and social species. Are there more social factors that come into play? Are there individual differences in our relationship with high-rise living?

Many assume that high-rise living makes us less content, but is this backed up by significant evidence – and can we make generalisations for all types of people?

## Satisfaction, home attachment and social contact

A standout study from the 1980s compared the psychological effects of living in three-storey and fourteen-storey public housing projects in New York. The local authority had assigned families to either type of building as vacancies arose, creating a natural randomisation. The families that ended up in the two building types did not differ much in their demographics. Nevertheless, residents of the high-rise buildings reported greater feelings of alienation and less satisfaction with their building. This is perhaps down to the lack of opportunity to meet others, which in turn leads to a mistrust of people from different backgrounds, who are typically brought together in such buildings.

Such disenfranchisement is likely to be reflected in the higher rate of turnover of residents in high-rise housing: research in the US reveals that, for people of moderate incomes, turnover is greater in this type of housing than in terraced houses or low-rise apartments. Subjective feelings of attachment to high-rise homes are lower than in low-rise homes, and it is self-evident that subjective attachment will correlate with how long you stay in a place. Research shows that this effect holds true irrespective of your life stage, education and income.

## Individual differences

While these studies suggest a decrease in satisfaction on average, there are important individual differences that influence satisfaction. In a nationwide survey of twenty-three urban centres in Canada, satisfaction reduced for high-rise residents only if they owned their home, but for those who rented, the height of the building made no difference at all. This could be explained simply by the argument that if you don't own a home you don't allow yourself to become so attached to it, and if you don't become too attached you won't be too troubled by its shortcomings. Perhaps not surprisingly, personality is another mediating influence. In a study of fresher students placed randomly in high- and low-rise accommodation, only those students who rated themselves as more extrovert or 'socially competent' were much disaffected by living in higher-rise dormitories. For those who were more introverted, the height of their dorm made little difference.

Another personality factor that can influence satisfaction with tower blocks is neuroticism. If you are more prone to low moods and emotional distress, you will be more distressed by high-rise as opposed to low-rise living. If the block has a higher density of people living in it, the effect on stress levels for the neurotic is even higher.

This analysis highlights an important third factor – the amount and quality of social contact in the building. The higher up you live, the more neighbours you know (perhaps from meeting them in the lift) but the fewer you know *well*. Those who live lower down have better social networks. (It follows that being isolated on the top floor would be more distressing for an extrovert than an introvert.) This is not just because those on lower floors spend more time with their neighbours within the same building; it has also been shown that they spend more time with others at street level. This echoes what we discovered about neighbourhood in the last chapter: the more we connect with people in our immediate environment, the more we connect beyond it.

It is easy to draw a parallel with the research findings from low-rise neighbourhoods – that there is a decrease in satisfaction with increased distance from a street. This relationship seems to hold true in both the vertical and horizontal planes of our existence.

We know that having a social network buffers against stress and negative moods, so it would not be surprising if the relative lack of relationships higher up were to cause us to feel less content. It is also an interesting insight that people who live on higher floors are less likely to exercise. Although they have access to a lift, it is as if the slightly greater time and effort required to get to street level is enough to tip the balance toward inaction. This then deprives them of yet another proven buffer against stress, anxiety and depression – vigorous physical exertion.

## Streets in the sky

In order to compensate for the fact that high-rise flats are remote from normal streets, architects have endeavoured to create communal passageways, built into the fabric of the building. One of the earliest examples of high-rise streets can be found in Le Corbusier's Unité d'habitation in Marseille, built over sixty years ago (see opposite).

Its internal 'streets' are of a good size, and include a doctor's surgery, some shops and a restaurant. When I visited I found the little restaurant and bar charming, but the streets themselves lacked natural light.

They are little more than generously proportioned corridors and, unfortunately, that is how they feel. The concrete roof garden, one of the first of its kind, has a paddling pool and great views of the sea. However, again it seems to lack the most basic human of needs – naturalness and sense of place. In the height of summer – on my visit – it was deserted.

Le Corbusier's Unité d'habitation, Marseille

It occurred to me that this building, held up as one of the more successful of the high-rises, was actually just a museum, lived in proudly by its mostly successful middle-class residents, who tended to do their socialising elsewhere, probably in a normal street.

In Robin Hood Gardens in London, the decks that ran alongside its rows of flats never really felt like proper streets. This was because they were not particularly generous. Even when wider streets were built which could take cars, like in the huge (now listed) Park Hill estate in Sheffield (see overleaf), these were only ever half a street, because they were on the exterior of a block, not enclosed by properties on either side. In the case of Robin Hood Gardens the view from the 'streets' was either of a busy road or a featureless central garden.

Park Hill estate, Sheffield

Why does this matter? Well, first of all, raised streets with a sheer drop on one side (albeit with barriers) don't feel secure, and not just because of their height. A normal street feels secure because one side can keep an eye on the other. Also, the two-sided street encourages more casual social contact.

### Lack of gardens

So, we have considered how living high up might make us more prone to stress, and even ill health, and how this is in part because of the lack of ready access to a street. However, the lack of direct access to a private garden is also important, particularly for certain groups. In 1972, a study carried out by the Department of the Environment in the UK examined the effects of mothers with young children being placed in council flats above ground level. They chose six council estates (or projects) located in London and Sheffield for the study. Four-fifths of all the women surveyed were unperturbed about living high up, but housewives with young children hated it, irrespective of the height above the ground. They wanted a house with a garden.

The psychologist Christopher Bagley was interested in whether this frustrated need in young mothers led to an increase in stress-related mental health problems. He compared young mothers with the same demographic backgrounds who had been allocated to either high-rise flats or semi-detached council houses. The latter group had fewer neurotic symptoms and visited their GP less often for 'nervous illness'.

Bagley surmised that it was the lack of private garden facilities for the children to play in that was the main determinant of the high neuroticism scores, although there was a contribution of stress from traffic noise at lower levels. Having a job to go to during the day helped to provide some buffer against the stress of high-rise parenting.

A bigger study of GP medical records revealed that housing stress is increased in families even if they are just a few storeys above the ground. A study of 558 families of British servicemen based in Germany was carried out by the psychologist Fanning. The families had been randomly assigned to houses or flats in blocks of up to thee or four storeys. The overall illness rate for the families in flats was 57 per cent higher than for those in the houses, while the rate of neurosis was *eight times* higher. The study was important, because although the level of neurosis was highest in women with children, it was also significantly high in women per se. There is something stressful about being deprived of private outside space – a consequence of being in a flat, irrespective of how high up it is. However, this does not mean that the neurosis would not have been even higher had high-rise blocks been included. The highly influential architect Christopher Alexander reviewed the evidence in his book *A Pattern Language*, and warned that, irrespective of age and gender: 'The higher people live off the ground, the more likely they are to suffer mental illness.'

There are important caveats here. A lot of the research evidence has been derived from situations where high-rise homes have been allocated to people on lower incomes. Residents had no choice in the matter. As alluded to in the introduction to this book, people who have more money and who choose to live in high-rise blocks might well be happier in them. Bagley conducted a study of patients on a psychiatric ward. He found that recent migration had been a major factor in triggering their illness, but this population was also more likely to have been allocated to social housing in a high-rise block. As we have seen with our discussion of identity, much of the stress we feel in a city home comes from a lack of choice over where we live, the type of housing we live in, who we live with, and how we furnish our living spaces.

It is important to consider individual differences in income, stage of life and gender. Wealthy single males, for example, might thrive in well-equipped high-rise blocks in the heart of London or Manhattan. When comparing stress levels in high- and low-rise buildings, allowance must be made for any selection bias. It is true to say that many city dwellers are indifferent to the height they live above the ground.

Nevertheless, there are definitely some specific design failings in many high-rise buildings which cause avoidable housing stress. A review of the most recent research on factors affecting mental health in high-rise residents was presented at the 43rd Conference of the Environmental Design Research Association in May 2012. Marwa Abdelman and Kristi Gaines of Texas Tech University presented on 'Inside high rise living: Effects on mental health', drawing attention to two main types of problems: structural and non-structural stressors.

The structural stressors included reduced access to sunlight; light pollution from street lights and advertising boards; increased traffic and street noise (high-rises are often positioned by busy roads); traffic vibration; and poor ventilation. In cities with a high density of high-rises, such as Hong Kong, residents living on the lower floors are starved of sunlight – this, not surprisingly, leads to more sadness and fatigue, and an increased risk of clinical depression. They are, in effect, prone to something akin to Seasonal Affective Disorder, or Winter Depression, as experienced in northern latitudes – the cure for which is exposure to bright light. It is obviously not possible to move the buildings further apart, but some cunning adaptations can be made: reflectors have been successfully used to redirect some of the sunlight from higher floors to the lower ones. Alternatively, individual flats can be fitted with reflectors extending out from their living-room windows, with mirrors oriented at 45°.

Residents of high-rises often complain that their flats are too stuffy, usually because they lack ventilation between floors. This is a necessary feature of high-rise construction: if all the heat arising from all the stacked-up people living below was allowed to travel upwards, the convection winds would be extreme. Solutions include a window with a view that can be opened for much of the day, and/or air-conditioning.

Non-structural stressors were factors not related to the actual structure of the building, but included some of the main social and psychological factors we have already considered. These can be grouped under three main categories:

1. The perception of hazards. As Robert Gifford suggested, many residents do, in fact, fear dying due to earthquakes or fires, or falling from windows or balconies, but this tends to be true only for temporary residents or those not living in a high-rise by choice.

2. Lack of social networks, in turn influenced by the context of the tower block. Social networks were reduced when the pavements were considered unsafe. Geographic isolation was also a factor leading to a fear of crime and anonymity.

3. Crowding. Mean-sized corridors and foyers that are 'double loaded' (where residents of two opposite blocks of flats exit on to it) can lead to antisocial behaviour. Within an arrangement of a floor, and within a flat, having more interconnected spaces and interconnected routes increases social interaction. High-rises often have limited aspects of both.

## Feeling exposed

Another aspect of design that can cause distress is apparent when high buildings are clustered together. For example, residents in the expensive new NEO Bankside apartments on the South Bank in London have complained that people are using the viewing gallery of the nearby Tate Modern gallery extension to look into their homes (see opposite).

This was met with a glib response from Sir Nicholas Serota, the outgoing director of the Tate, who suggested that the residents put up lace curtains. In effect, Serota was arguing that choosing to live in transparency means exhibiting yourself to the world – so do not be surprised if the rest of the world looks back. This is the problem of the high-rise which is often ignored, by both developers and residents. You might be afforded fabulous expanses of glass with the luxury of panoramic views, but with a view out, there is a view back in.

The overlooked NEO Bankside apartments and Tate modern extension, London

What is at first regarded as a luxury soon becomes a source of stress, as Edith Farnsworth discovered (see Chapter 1). She felt uneasy living in her glass box, even though it was positioned in the Illinois countryside. If you move into an apartment in the NEO Bankside, or worse still, on the tightly clustered high-rises that are proposed for the Nine Elms development which will span the riversides of Vauxhall and Battersea in London, you are likely to experience the same unease.

## Living next to a high-rise

Although there has been plenty of research on the impact of high-rise living on its inhabitants, there is less information on what impacts high-rise blocks have on the surrounding neighbourhood, including the street life.

One study of Elahieh in Tehran found that a proliferation of high-rises (housing a total of 5,000 residents) had a significant negative impact on livability for the streets where they were located. The impacts included a lack of sunlight, shadows over important public or private places, a change in wind behaviour, loss of character in the neighbourhood by encouraging more commercial development, increased congestion on local streets, visual disruption and a negative effect on pedestrian life.

The canyon-like effect of the tall structures increased wind speeds by three to four times. Numerous underground-parking entrances opened out onto one narrow road. The towers blocked views of the surrounding Alborz mountains to the north, which is considered to be the only pleasing view from the city. Many people described a feeling of enclosure, and a lack of access to the streetscape. They disliked the fact that the new high-rise blocks were not sensitive to context, not fitting in with the older buildings they abutted.

The high-rise blocks did not provide adequate pedestrian connection to the surrounding urban area, because their only function was residential. There was no real connection to the street because there were no shops, offices or other business on the ground level. As such, they created a dead area. Not all high-rises are like this. Many planners and architects are now understanding the importance of communicating with street life because it's better for the street as well as for the residents living higher up. They might also make attempts to step a new tower block back from the street, creating a public space. When this happens, the pedestrian does not feel dominated by the enormity of the structure, while the street itself feels less closed-in – it has space to breathe.

# Chapter 13

# Making better high-rises

As our cities become ever more populated, high-rise buildings are increasingly seen as the answer to providing more living space, but they can blight the lives of people living in them and around them. What is needed is attention to aspects of the design that allow for access to private open spaces, the street and other people – through horizontal and vertical connections. The tower block does not exist in isolation – it stands over the rest of the neighbourhood, the building next door and the person on the street. From the ground up, the monolithic nature of the typical high-rise is intimidating and dehumanising. It needs to be more sensitive to the surrounding area, less confrontational.

The Israeli architect Moshe Safdie has spent much of his career trying to achieve just that. The façades of his high-rises are broken up by a process that he calls 'fractalisation'. The word 'fractal' is derived from the Latin *fractus*, meaning broken or fractured. There are many different types of fractal, which create a wide variety of the geometric patterns seen in nature. The Mandelbrot set is a good example.

Safdie's high-rise buildings are broken into similarly irregular fragments. These fragments are arranged like leaves on a tree, to allow for each flat to have maximum exposure to sunlight, and his stepped façades turn in different directions to benefit further from this. Increasing complexity in this way not only increases access to light but it is more visually appealing. Evidence suggests that fractal shapes, and increased complexity in high-rise façades, increase their acceptability to the general population.

Moshe Safdie's Habitat 67, Montreal

He recognises that towers do not 'function as freestanding objects' but have an effect on the surrounding area – casting shadows, blocking light, causing wind tunnels and intimidating life on the street. His first attempt at fractilising the high-rise building was Habitat 67 in Montreal (see above), Canada, constructed of rambling prefabricated building blocks, each with perforations of space in between, and each with their own bits of outside space.

Although Habitat 67 was popular among its inhabitants, the design never proliferated. Perhaps it challenged the prevailing style too much.

## Gardens in the sky

Bedok Court in Singapore signalled a new form of high-rise living. It incorporated 'tropical courtyards' at every level, one for each flat. Large airwells were provided between the courtyards. The corridors linking the apartments mimicked the streets of a *kampong*, with views of these courtyards all along them – so-called 'tropical streets in the sky'. (A *kampong* is a village, but the term is often used both for slums and for developments within cities, and these are highly sociable.)

Compared to the open decks or balconies that were provided in older high-rises, these planted spaces afforded more visual and social contact with other residents. They were well cared for and there was evidence of their use as real recreational spaces. Individuals became more attached to their homes because they could adapt their outside spaces to suit them, and create a sense of place. Unlike decks and corridors, these gardens in the sky had a sense of ownership, each with their unique identity, and together they created to a sense of varied street life that might be found in a *kampong*. In other words, they were meaningful places, the whole community able to identify with them. They also provided the visual complexity and contact with nature that time and again has been shown to be satisfying and restorative. The overlapping nature of the courtyards allowed some visual connection vertically as well as horizontally, potentially providing even more connectedness than is achieved by a traditional street.

Bedok Court has since influenced even more impressive experiments with elevated green spaces. A complex of skyscrapers called Bosco Verticale (see below) was recently opened in Milan with the aim of constructing a vertical forest right in the centre of the city. Eight hundred trees and 4,000 shrubs were planted for the project.

The Rødovre Skyscraper in Copenhagen is not yet built but will lean northwards in order that a variety of terraced sky gardens will be south-facing, making the most of the sun. The stacked neighbourhood, or Sky Village, could become a model for the future of high-rise living.

Bosco Verticale, Milan

The provision of elevated gardens not only improves the satisfaction of most residents, it also makes life easier for the parents of small children. They provide a safe place for them to play, within close sight.

Safdie's most recent efforts to reinvent the tower block set new standards for high-density living in places where land is scarce. His more recent projects are truly impressive ladders to the heavens, with sky gardens on every level.

## Understand the headspace of high-rise living

The weight of scientific evidence suggests that high-rise buildings have a negative effect on our mental wellbeing, whether we live in them or next to them. This has big implications for town planning and individual choice. Ideally, cities might follow the guidance of the influential architect Christopher Alexander decades ago: keep the majority of buildings four storeys high or less, and if you have to make a building higher, make sure it is never used for human habitation.

There are big caveats, of course. There is no doubt that some people like living in high-rise blocks – especially if they have chosen to do so. We know that high-rises definitely do not suit women with young children. However, extroverts, temporary renters, artists and young people are likely to fare better. We need to think about how different people at different life stages suit different types of housing. When reviewing the evidence, it seems that it is the youngest and oldest who prefer to live centrally and in high-rises, while people with families prefer to live away from the centre of cities. Younger adults focus on social life, but individuals in midlife want to pursue other interests, such as gardening, which are not compatible with high-rise living. The architect and psychologist Roberta Feldman found, after interviewing the inhabitants of Chicago and Denver, that most of us conform to one of three sub-strata of society:

1. City people regard themselves as urban pioneers, who value diversity and vibrant communities

2. Suburbanites value privacy, safety and closeness to nature
3. Country dwellers value a simple way of life

Of these 'settlement stereotypes' it is the young and single urban pioneers who are the best fit for the high-rise apartment. Nevertheless, some high-rises cause unnecessary stress by virtue of the location and design. If, in our rapidly growing cities, we must build up, then we can heed the lessons of badly designed tower blocks. Individuals living in well-designed middle-income high-rise blocks in New York report high levels of satisfaction. Safdie's more humane skyscrapers provide a good model for reducing their potential negative impact on the surrounding city while providing more personal outside spaces and inviting places to meet neighbours, as well as better access to the light and air we crave. The best examples connect properly with the street, while being more sensitive to life at ground level. Anyone who chooses to live above the ground should heed the lessons of the research and choose wisely.

Part Five

# Public Places: Places for Play

In the last two chapters we looked at what makes for a thriving and satisfying neighbourhood: a neighbourhood that promotes social contact and a sense of belonging, while avoiding the stress of noise pollution and heavy traffic. We touched on the importance of ownership and sense of place, and how these ideas extended from our homes to the main street and the public spaces close to our homes. In the ideal walkshed community, these nearby spaces would include places for recreation and play – for adults and their children.

Play is a physical or mental leisure activity that is undertaken purely for enjoyment or amusement. It has no other objective, and that is the beauty of it. However, without the opportunity to play – alone and with others – we do not develop properly as children. Play is essential for us to develop motor coordination, problem-solving and social skills. Children instinctively want (and need) to play with others – it is imperative for their development. Playing with others is a behaviour that is unique to mammals, perhaps because we have always needed to form groups to survive. Learning the skills of negotiation and cooperation is as important now as it was in the ancestral environment.

Chapter 14

# Child's play

What are the best environments in which to play? Simply, they are places with lots of visual interest. Put a child in a place that feeds their imagination, and they will explore it. There is a growing amount of evidence to suggest that natural settings are the most stimulating, which provides a challenge in a densely populated city. It is concerning that an increasing number of children never come into contact with nature. Not only does that restrict their development, but it also deprives them of any knowledge of nature, and therefore any sense of responsibility to preserve it. The reasons for children staying indoors are many, but include both parents working long hours and the unsupervised use of digital technology – computers, tablets and smartphones.

In his book *Last Child in the Woods*, the American journalist Richard Louv gathered together a large catalogue of research evidence to show that a nature-deficient childhood leads to attention disorders (like ADHD), obesity, a dampening of creativity and even depression. He summarises this rag-bag of psychological ailments as a Nature Deficit Disorder. The problem, he argues, is on the increase. The prescribed cure is for children to be forced to make contact with other living things – once they are placed in a natural environment they instinctively engage with it over time, exploring how other creatures live.

Children exhibit more creative play in outdoor spaces with more vegetation than in more barren outdoor spaces, and it has been shown that these green spaces can reduce some of the symptoms of attention deficit disorder (ADD). The accessibility of vegetation buffers against the impact of life stressors for children in the same way as it does for adults, through providing a retreat. However, there are probably indirect effects on stress that are due to the social benefits of being in nature: children in rural natural settings are drawn together because exploring nature provides a context for creating friendships. In turn, the increased social support is thought to buffer against the impact of stressful life events.

If green space is limited in our neighbourhood, how do we provide a similar level of stimulation? The answer is in the careful design of playgrounds. Dr Magdalena Czalczynska-Podolska, of the West Pomeranian University of Technology (ZUT) in Szczecin, Poland, explored this issue by comparing child behaviour in ten contemporary public playgrounds in the South Bay area of California. In her review she observed how the best playgrounds supported physical, social, emotional and cognitive development.

She found that playground features with a high degree of variety and curiosity – such as the more complex climbing and slide structures – were very effective in enticing children to start playing. In order to encourage children to interact with one another, hiding places underneath objects were particularly effective. What they offered was a kind of semiprivate domain where kids could pair off and explore. So, although it seems paradoxical, playgrounds that offered a lot of enclosed spaces encouraged more social play. They might also satisfy the human instinct for mystery – a recurring theme throughout this book.

Another important generator of play was about providing things that children could shape and transform themselves. Sand pits and ponds were much more popular than static objects like wooden horses and miniature houses. For example, sand could be combined with water to make sand castles. This fits nicely with the consistent finding that children play more in natural environments than in urban playgrounds. In nature they have an abundant amount of material to work with – sand, mud, sticks, grass, pinecones and so on. At a beach or in a forest, play is infinitely flexible because of the variety and flexibility of things to explore and manipulate. It is not surprising that bringing some of this nature into a playground is successful.

As in nature, variety was the most important characteristic of the playground in encouraging play. The more diverse were the places to play, the stronger was their influence over participation, and it was best when they were close to each other, or linked in some way. For example, sand pits were used much more if they had a water feature nearby. When play components like swings and roundabouts were closer together, this encouraged children to carry out activities in loops. Children spent more time on linked structures than on separated ones. Playgrounds that were too large, where play components were too separate or too far apart, 'disturbed the natural sequence of the play pattern'. In smaller playgrounds with well-linked zones and a clear path from one zone to another, play developed more readily, and the amount of play increased – both solitary and group play.

Again, natural elements rise to the top of what makes us happy – the best playground is a natural one. Cities like London and San Francisco have wilder, less tended parks, and urban forests. The next-best thing is a playground with a variety of things to explore, as in nature, and which allows children to create their own games. Children need safe places to play, away from traffic. One study documented that four-year-olds who could not play independently outdoors, primarily because of the threat of traffic, had more strained relations with their parents, had fewer playmates, and manifested poorer emotional and social development.

Jane Jacobs, in her book *The Death and Life of Great American Cities* set out some guiding principles for meeting children's needs in the urban environment, many of which have been supported by research. These included:

1. Schools, libraries and other formal services that children can access themselves
2. Buildings of different eras
3. Rugged open spaces for exploration
4. Broad pavements by quieter roads
5. Provision of playgrounds and sports fields
6. Vegetation and wildlife
7. Sites for fairs and circuses

A well-designed school is not just for classroom learning, it has an important role in encouraging play. In Japan, Takaharu Tezuka and his wife Yui, who make up Tezuka Architects, build schools that are centred on trees and known for their generous play spaces. These show what can be achieved through careful planning. They also hint at how existing schools might be adapted to provide even better play spaces for our children.

The Fuji Kindergarten in Tachikawa, near Tokyo, completed in 2007, cunningly uses the roof of the school as a huge playground. The roof is wide and circular, allowing the children infinite space to run around (see below). According to the architects, '... the roof provides further support for the observation that children love to run around in circles'. Amazingly, the children of this school walk or run an average of 4,000 metres in one day. The architects proudly announced that the pupils of this kindergarten were the most athletic in Tokyo. Another benefit is that there is no corner where the children can feel trapped.

The flat roof of the Fuji Kindergarten in Tachikawa, Tokyo

There are other thoughtful design aspects. For example, the circular roof is not so high that adults cannot see the children from the central space below, and children can sit and watch a performance in this space. The second notable feature is that the classroom spaces under the roof are open to the central courtyard for most of the year, with no barrier between inside and outside. Each classroom has at least one skylight to enhance the feeling of light and space. Some children become nervous and disruptive when kept confined within a room, so the open design is calming. Also, children who become overstimulated can leave the classroom space easily, until they have calmed down.

Thirdly, there are places to explore that have some element of danger built in. The large roof is penetrated by trees growing through it in places, with rope netting around them, to provide contact with nature and a little sense of danger. The children learn to help each other to navigate the trees and other interesting wooden structures carefully placed around. Overall, the design of the school is successful because it does not control or confine its children, or dictate how they play. It lets them explore and roam free. It allows them to tumble sometimes, and learn from the experience – a critical function of play. Once again, the opportunity to explore nature is critical to the school's success, and explains why the architects always build their schools around mature trees.

The need for play and learning continues into adult life. It keeps us vital. It fires our imagination and creativity, and at its most rewarding it brings us together with others in cooperation. So, what features of a public space can encourage play in the city?

Adult play can happen in the garden, shed, street, college, sports club, theatre, music venue, art gallery, restaurant, café, pub or bar. It can happen in a square, park or pop-up venue in the nooks and crannies of the city. All we need is some like-minded people and a lack of formality. However, it seems that, as with children, we are at our freest in a natural setting.

Chapter 15

# Adults are kids, too: green spaces

All fields we'll turn to sports grounds, lit at night
From concrete standards with fluorescent light.
And all over the land, instead of trees
Clean poles and wires will whisper in the breeze.

*Planter's Vision* (1970), John Betjeman

It is not a coincidence that the most popular cities in the world have a lot of green space. London has more parks than any other city, and they are incredibly popular. Like many successful parks around the world, their landscapes all meet the requirements defined by Ulrich in Chapter 1 for a satisfying view: they have smooth ground cover, scattered trees, some openness and depth, and water features. They also have parts that are wild, or obscured, and land that rises up and falls away. Although Hyde Park, with its 3,000 trees and Serpentine lake is most visited, it is arguably the wildest parks that are most invigorating and restorative. Hampstead Heath has fields to run in, long grass to roll in, woods to hide in and, most famously, ponds to swim in. C.S. Lewis lived near Hampstead Heath. Its rises, ponds and woodland glades are thought to have inspired his vision of Narnia.

Hordes flock to the refreshing waters of the Heath's celebrated ponds in the summer months, and in the colder months it's more rewarding to while away an afternoon feeding the ducks or exploring the lush woodland, bogs, hedgerows and grassland. London's councils make sure that the parks host events year-round: sports events, open-air theatre, food festivals, art fairs and live music concerts that give them a sense of place. Their differing forms encourage different activities. The flatness of Clapham Common makes it popular for team sports and jogging. Over just a few years the Common has developed its own unofficial running track.

## Buffering against stress

Agnes van den Berg, professor of Experiencing and Valuing Nature and Landscape at the University of Groningen in Holland, has conducted a series of experiments examining how green space near to where we live can reduce the impact of stress – through a buffering effect.

As she observes, we often seek out nature in times of stress. For example, US national parks observed a pronounced increase in the number of visits following the attacks on the World Trade Center, New York in 2001. Park managers noted that people were not just wandering aimlessly but were using the space and time to reflect on what had happened.

Public parks can support physical activity and facilitate social cohesion. However, according to Professor van den

Berg, green spaces appear to have a special quality that is lacking in other public areas: national surveys in several countries have consistently shown that being in nature is one of the most powerful ways for people to obtain relief from stress.

A study in Helsinki, Finland, found that even short visits to an urban park or an urban woodland led to marked stress-relieving effects in city dwellers (when compared with a visit to the city centre). They also found reduced levels of the stress hormone cortisol in their saliva – disrupted patterns of cortisol secretion over the course of a day are associated with poor mental and physical health. Cortisol has been shown to be sensitive to activities in natural environments in many studies. For example, if you take male university students to forest and city environments, away from their usual work or home contexts, their cortisol levels will drop. When people who engaged in gardening as a hobby in their local allotments were asked to spend time either gardening or reading indoors, the former reduced their cortisol more than the latter.

Research has seldom attempted to detect a biological impact of exposure to green and natural environments encountered as part of 'everyday life', especially for deprived urban populations, who are generally exposed to more stress. A study in Dundee, Scotland examined changes in cortisol throughout the day in people who were not working, for whatever reason (unemployed, on incapacity benefit, caring for a family member and so on). It found that the greater the amount of time for which people were exposed to green areas in a day, the lower was their cortisol as the day went on. Those who did not have much exposure to greenery but did plenty of exercise also had reduced cortisol levels, demonstrating that exercise helps compensate for a lack of green space in combating stress.

In this study, the amounts of green space were not copious. In general, the scientific evidence suggests that we do not need to have wilderness on our doorsteps to feel the benefit of contact with other living things. Although seascapes and other wild open spaces are optimal, we can still feel restoration in the bits of green that a city can offer, if care is taken to expose ourselves to it. We can also ensure that more trees are planted, that we plant more shrubs and green verges along our roads.

Professor van den Berg points out that our instinctive attraction to nature is expressed in how effortlessly our attention is held by natural scenes – what Rachel Kaplan called a 'soft fascination'. When nature captures people's attention, pessimistic thoughts are blocked, and negative emotions are replaced by positive ones. Beyond this immediate effect, spending a longer time in natural landscapes gives us space to contemplate bigger life questions, make sense of where we are and what direction our life should take next. This is the goal of the Native American tradition of the Vision Quest – a solitary journey into the wilderness for several days, where the wanderer communes with nature and reassesses priorities, goals and their own place in the larger scheme of things. These rituals often occur at major transitions in life, including coming-of-age.

However, the power of nature to inspire change does not appear to be true of all landscapes. Idit Shalev of Ben-Gurion University in Israel explored the effect of pictures, both real and imagined, of arid landscapes. From an evolutionary point of view, deserts are less favourable to wellbeing and survival. In this study, viewing pictorial images or visualising mental images of a desert (versus a landscape with water or a control) felt more stressful and 'depleting'. In other words, desert images reduced feelings of vitality. In turn this reduced participants' confidence in their ability to change negative habits and addictions, like smoking.

Interestingly, viewing a desert was still better for feelings of vitality than viewing an urban scene, devoid of any nature. The scene with water increased motivation for change at the same time as increasing subjective vitality.

In general, research has shown that positive emotional and cognitive effects can be obtained from nearby green space such as gardens as well as more remote settings. Even looking through a window can be helpful. Office workers in southern Europe were less likely to experience work stress and quit their jobs if they had a view of nature.

Green space may not only affect stress and mental fatigue directly in the moment, but may, over time, build up some immunity to the impact of a stressful life event, such as a bereavement or a major health crisis like being diagnosed with cancer. Research in Sweden has shown that daily exposure to nature improves mental health and attention in response to such personal crises.

So, adult play in green spaces makes us happier, aids contemplation, helps us deal with major negative life events, and buffers against stress, while encouraging social contact. Merely being exposed to views of nature might be enough to keep us free of mental distress a lot of the time, but travelling to larger, wilder spaces will be more helpful at times of severe stress. When travelling out of the city limits is not possible, being next to a park is a priority. The more parks that we can create from the disused parts of our cities, the less stressed we all will be.

## Greening up New York

Amanda Burden, New York's chief city planner in 2002–13 under the Bloomberg administration, led the revitalisation of some of the city's most familiar features – from the High Line to the Brooklyn waterfront. Quality public places give residents the opportunity to play, to assemble and to take more pride in their neighbourhoods. It might sound obvious, but providing good public places where people are encouraged to meet is what makes a city work. Without them, a city is lifeless.

Public space is not given high priority when land is scarce and expensive. As ordinary citizens we have no idea just how much pressure business exerts on city planners – commercial interests bring more money into the city and it can be too tempting to concede to them.

Burden has never succumbed. New York has been improved because she has stood up to big business and made her case for longer-term benefits. By creating lively, enjoyable public places from disused rail lines, waterfronts and abandoned factories, she has transformed a lot of Manhattan and Brooklyn into areas where people want to live, eat, drink and shop. It's a win-win.

She has been successful because she has done her homework on what makes a good public space, and she has strongly argued that the self-esteem of a city is more important in the long term than short-term commercial gains. She takes 'the long view for the common good'. Public spaces have the power to make us feel good. As Burden says, 'People feel better about their city just knowing that they are there. A successful city is like a fabulous party. People stay because they are having a good time.'

The best public space is inviting by its very nature. It doesn't put up any boundaries or barriers, or if it does these are permeable – we can see through them or over them and find a way around them. People pass through it, and stay if they want to; they come and go as they please. Burden observed the behaviour of people in Paley Park, a small pocket park in Manhattan: things that made it a success included comfortable, moveable chairs and abundant greenery, but most of all, it was accessible – people didn't feel as if they were trespassing.

These successes do not come about by accident; they arise from putting human needs first. As Burden articulates: 'Would you want to go there? Can you see into it or out of it? Does it seem green and friendly? Are there other people? Are there street cafés?'

In contrast, the bleak plazas of developers that protrude from large office or residential blocks look desolate and actually feel dangerous. They suit the owners of these buildings because they deter any undesirables and they are low-maintenance, but they take up space that could be used to make us feel happier about being in the city. Developers should be forced to be provide inviting places to sit – spaces for recreation.

Bad developments like this can be become a thing of the past, according to Burden. If we start with a good park, good developments will then grow around it, as she proved when she developed Battery Park on the southern tip of Manhattan island in the 1980s. Good parks like this are designed around people, with great attention to detail. During the design process, the mile-long esplanade was first mocked up in wood, with many places to sit. It soon became clear that the esplanade's waterside railing was blocking the view when people were seated. The railing was redesigned so that it no longer spoilt the view. The planting of trees and plants was planned according to the feedback from visitors to this prototype park. The lighting was designed to avoid any dark spaces so that the park felt safe.

Burden was also responsible for greening up the degraded waterfronts at Williamsburg and Green Point. Tree-lined paths now invite people from the upland to the waterside. There are lots of places to rest, including bar seating right on the river. The waterfront railing widens at points where seating is provided so that people have a surface for eating or working on their laptops in summer.

At first, Burden had to face concerns about the amount of money that was to be spent clearing up such undesirable neighbourhoods. The prevailing view was that no one would ever visit or inhabit these areas, but she proved the doubters wrong: if you build a good park, the people will come. And come they did, in their thousands, from all over the city. A new ferry service runs between Brooklyn and Lower Manhattan, and it is used daily by the residents of Brooklyn and the visitors from Manhattan – as if the park, and the community springing up around it, had always been there.

Probably the most famous Burden project is the High Line: a park that now runs the length of the disused raised train line on Manhattan's West Side (see opposite). Four million people visit it every year in order to get their fix of nature, escape from the traffic and bustle below, and take in new views of the city. Crucially it is important to note that Burden does not just stick new public places anywhere. She puts them in development zones. Since 2002, 90 per cent of any new development has been within a ten-minute walk of a subway. There is no need to own a car, you can walk to your nearest open space – an ambitious attempt to create a walkshed life for the people of NYC. Collectively, these new parks have

changed how New Yorkers see their city and its river –
from a city in decline to one of growth and vitality.

Not only should we push for more public space where
it is lacking, we should get involved when existing space
is threatened. For example, the High Line had to be
battled for, section by section, and is still under pressure
from retailers to take out the old plantings and install
shops along the side; but as Burden has pointed out, 'This
would not be a park, it would be a Mall . . . Public spaces
always need vigilant protection.'

It does not take much research to know that city
areas with parks are preferred over places that haven't.
Top of the 50 Most Livable Neighborhoods in New York,
according to *nymag.com*, was Park Slope in Brooklyn.
It was placed top of the list partly because of the 'vast
stretches of green space'.

The High Line, New York

## Urban planting

Where spaces for parks are limited, much can be done to 'green up' a drab grey neighbourhood by using the right plants and innovative planting techniques. This is a topic that has, for the past thirty years, preoccupied Professor James Hitchmough of Sheffield University, who also co-designed the Southern Hemisphere Garden in London's Olympic Park. Motivated by improving the wellbeing of urban dwellers, he is interested not only in the sustainability and ecology of urban plants but also in what patterns of planting are most pleasing to the human eye. Starting his work in the grasslands near Melbourne, Australia, he has brought wild meadows into the city, gradually learning why some urban plantings thrive and some die, and how to control the growth of different plants, so that the overall effect is balanced. It all comes down to the mini-ecosystem you create. His methods allow control over the density of different plant species within a layered, textured group. The theme of complexity within order comes to the fore again, with beautiful results.

Through his studies of natural habitats, Hitchmough has learnt which plants grow well together, and also developed ways to genetically engineer plants to thrive on rubble and other hard urban surfaces, in the cold and the wet, and by the roadside. Sometimes a base matrix is created for the plants to grow on, which needs little maintenance, achieving a wild, natural effect. These important developments show us ways to incorporate nature back into our urban worlds.


## Blue spaces

So far we have looked at the power of green spaces to rejuvenate us during adult play, but as we learnt in the first chapter, parks that are most preferred have water in them. Dr Herzog of the Grand Valley State College in Michigan has found a straightforward positive relationship between the amount of water there is in a landscape and how much we like it. Mountain lakes are preferred over rivers, which are in turn preferred over ponds and swamps.

Water is animated and alive, constantly varying on its surface, and most of us find it captivating. From an evolutionary perspective the human attraction to water makes sense: fresh water is a necessary commodity for the preservation of life and so an instinctive preference for watery scenes confers a survival benefit. Seascapes are the most restorative of aquatic environments. One reason for their attraction could be their association with seafood. Omega-3 fatty acids, present in large amounts in fish and shellfish, may have played a crucial role in the development of the brain and the evolution of modern humans.

The aquatic ape hypothesis contends that in our evolutionary pasts we were forced to adapt to a semi-aquatic environment. Many justifications for this belief have been proposed – including bipedality, loss of hair, nose shape, design of sweat glands and the ability of babies to swim without drowning. One of the more convincing observations is the webbing between our fingers. There is no possible explanation for this other than to aid swimming, and so it is highly likely that at least some adaptation to watery environments has occurred in human history.

There are more prosaic explanations. Water invites interaction. You can literally immerse yourself in it. Even the mere act of floating in water, as in a flotation tank, has been shown to be restorative. Furthermore, just looking at water might evoke these calming responses vicariously. Also, the rhythmic sounds of water might be restorative, adding to the visual associations. If you doubt how much our species values water, you need only to look at the direct evidence of human behaviour: a study in Holland observed that people were prepared to spend more (8–12 per cent more) on property with a view of water. In the UK, there are 250 million visits to the coast every year, and 150 million to other bodies of water like lakes and rivers.

With these figures in mind, can water be restorative for city dwellers? Mathew White and his colleagues at Plymouth University conducted an interesting experiment looking at urban settings with and without water, and natural scenes with and without water; they also varied the amount of water. Their results lent further support to the notion that water can make any environment more likeable, and the same dose-response relationship came out, but with a few caveats.

The conclusions showed a nice trend in increasing preference as you move from scenes with no water to built environments with water and then to natural environments with water. However, it is interesting to note two exceptions. Firstly, urban environments with water were not significantly liked over entirely rural ones without water. Or, to put a more positive spin on it, putting water in a built environment pulled its likeability up to a par with an entirely natural scene. Secondly, for natural scenes containing water, more water increased liking, but there was a limit. Scenes consisting entirely of water were not liked as much as scenes with a bit of land in view. Again, this makes intuitive sense from an evolutionary point of view: to be situated in the middle of a large expanse of water with no sight of land might trigger fears of drowning.

The same researchers conducted a second experiment using simulated images of hotel rooms with different views. This time they asked the viewers how much they perceived the views to be restorative, and also how much they would be willing to pay (WTP) for the rooms. The WTP results chimed in with the preference results. Participants said they would pay the most for a natural view with water. However, the viewers perceived that a completely green scene was slightly more restorative than a built environment with water, no matter how much water was present. Taking the results of both experiments together, totally green spaces and urban spaces with water are roughly on a par in terms of their restorative power.

A really important message to come from this study is that, although built scenes containing some water were rated more positively than those without, the extra benefits of a greater proportion of water were relatively minimal. So, if we want to feel calmer in the city, just having a small water feature in view is enough to make a big difference.

Watery scenes are not just attractive to us, they reduce our stress levels, in common with green spaces. However, they probably have a more powerful effect on reducing stress levels: according to the European Centre for the Environment and Human Health, visits to the coast have been shown to be more stress-relieving than visits to forests and parks. Returning to the urban setting, Ulrich showed that pictures of watery scenes placed in offices reduced work-related stress.

If water reduces stress it might also be expected to improve our overall mental and physical health. Data from the English census of 2001 was used to test this hypothesis. Forty-eight million people took part, across 30,000 neighbourhoods. A group of researchers categorised these neighbourhoods by ease of access to the coast (e.g. 0–1 kilometres = walking distance; 2–5 kilometres = cycling/short drive distance, etc). They then looked for a relationship with responses to questions about health. Supporting the hypothesis, they found that the closer a neighbourhood was to the coast, the greater was the proportion of residents who rated their health as good. To give a feel of the size of the effect, the number reporting good health increased by only about one per cent as a result of living within 1 kilometre from the coast (compared with 50 kilometres away). You could argue that this effect is insignificant, but as the researchers point out, 1 per cent of 3 million is a lot of people.

When the effect of deprivation is considered, the results become more interesting. After stratifying the population by demographics, it turned out that the coastal effect was much stronger for people in impoverished communities – the people who have the worst health outcomes overall. If you are well off, your health is pretty good wherever you live. As we saw with studies of the effects of green space, the biggest influence over health was seen in poorer areas.

Population studies like this one, although interesting, run up against the problem of assuming that everyone in a group conforms to an average, but real life isn't like that: it's an 'ecological fallacy'. For example, extreme outliers in a community, who have very poor health, could disproportionately bring the average health down. It could be that most people have very good health. Or there might be an independent factor at play. Perhaps poorer areas tend to be the places where local authorities build their elderly care homes. The elderly individuals would skew the health stats toward the negative. The only real way to avoid the ecological fallacy is to conduct cohort studies –

looking at changes in the behaviour and health of a group over time. Ideally you would track the changing health of people who move from the city to the coast, and vice versa. One research project, using data from the British Household Panel Survey (BHPS), did just that.

The BHPS tracked the health of more than 5,000 households over seventeen years, collecting data every year from 1991 to 2008. Inevitably some people moved home during their participation in the panel survey, sometimes nearer to the coast and sometimes further from the coast.

So, the researchers were able to compare the self-reported health and mental wellbeing of people when they lived at different distances from the sea. More than 100,000 observations revealed that people reported better mental and physical health in the years when they lived closer to the sea. Again, although the absolute size of the coastal effect was small, it was not negligible. For example, being employed is known to have a big influence on health – being close to the coast had an effect that was over 20 per cent of that of having a job. This research was important in demonstrating positive impacts of coastal living on health while avoiding confounding factors, but more research is needed to explore what mechanisms might explain the effect.

The effect of blue and green spaces on health might be explained in part by the fact that they encourage exercise. We know that exercise improves health. However, there is something even more inspiring and restorative about interacting with natural spaces (running or wild swimming, for example) than just viewing them. They also encourage social interaction. This seems to be especially true for visits to the beach: in-depth interviews with fifteen families showed how much the children in particular regarded the beach as a place where all the family played together, and more freely than they did in a park. According to one eleven-year-old boy, 'Instead of the adults just sitting somewhere on a bench while the kids do activities, they get up and play frisbee or cricket and football and sometimes go swimming with them.'

A simple visit to the coast can provide much-needed stress relief as a result of contact with nature and the opportunity for exercise, but we can also think about what this research tells us about the cityscape. If we can't bring city dwellers to the coast, can we bring water to the city?


## A river runs through it

In fact, there are many projects around the world that are doing just that. Ellis Woodman, a critic for *The Architectural Review*, has explored the potential for urban rivers to rejuvenate a city and its population. Water is not just restorative, it also gives a city meaning: commonly a town or city has grown around a river, so bringing a river and its urban tributaries back to life restores the relationship between the inhabitants and their ancient waterways, between the people and their old means of trade with the rest of the country and the world. A city thrives when it recognises its past. As we have seen, a sense of history gives a place a soul.

The Moroccan architect Aziza Chaouni has fought to bring the Fez river back to life. Fez, her home city, grew up around the river, and this was once its lifeblood, once considered to represent its very soul. But over time, as the population grew, the city became stressed. The river was one of the victims of this. It succumbed to pollution – from human sewage and chemicals seeping from the tanneries. It began to give off a foul stench, and in the 1950s was covered over bit by bit by concrete slabs, until it was completely concealed from view. This was coupled with the destruction of houses along it – to allow larger vehicles to enter the narrow walled old town.

She learnt that the city had received a grant from central government to divert sewage away from the river, and treat it. With cleaner water flowing through the city, uncovering the river suddenly became possible. Slowly but surely she inspired the authorities to rehabilitate the waterway. Once the decision was made she worked tirelessly with engineers to uncover it, bit by bit. This rejuvenation had to go hand in hand with a dialogue with the people who lived and worked along it. To optimise the positive potential for their lives, she had to become an activist for the needs of the local population. Her ego as the author of the project had to be put in check.

In response to local needs, she filled the old voids caused by demolishing the homes with playgrounds and other public spaces. Walkways were returned to the river banks. Exhumed from its mummified state, it has once again become a source of restoration – an escape from the stresses of city life.

In London, its network of canals has been rediscovered and some of its waters have been redirected within the city to enhance its appearance. The old industrial wastelands of Hackney and King's Cross have been a major focus of rehabilitation. As well as reclaiming land for homes and leisure, a necklace of ancient waterways has been uncovered, and sometimes rerouted, softening the urban landscape and improving its livability.

A great example is Woodferry Down in Hackney. What has been uncovered includes a river originally intended to bring fresh water to the city from the chalk hills of the Chilterns. It was originally excavated through the wooded land of Stoke Newington in the seventeenth century, when it was known as the New River. Two large reservoirs were then built to store the water for drinking. Over the years the river and its bankside villas were neglected. Thames Water was threatening to sell off the reservoirs for housing. Then the fight back began. A strong campaign by the local residents saved the reservoirs. The West reservoir is now used as a sailing lake, while the East reservoir is a nature reserve, home to many herons.

The London Wildlife Trust conducted a pilot survey to gather information on the ponds and other wetlands in people's gardens and community spaces. Public perceptions of ponds were overwhelmingly positive: all but four out of more than 1,000 respondents with ponds were happy that they had a pond in their garden. What's more, 90 per cent recognised the benefit to their own sense of wellbeing.

The London Wildlife Trust and partners have installed a series of floating islands on the Regent's Canal in King's Cross, creating pockets of urban wetland habitat for London's wildlife. King's Cross is being transformed from an industrial wasteland to a restorative water-based haven for wildlife along its long-neglected waterways. The BioHaven islands contain wildflower meadows and habitats for birds. These play host to dragon flies and damselflies, and provide underwater shelters for fish. Such pockets of wildlife will provide a place for stressed-out Londoners to reconnect with nature and achieve some sense of calm.

The largest urban wetland park in Europe is to be created in the formerly undesirable area of Waltham Forest in London. The £6.5-million project will reinvent Walthamstow as a haven for wildlife, linking its ten

Victorian reservoirs by cycle paths, nature trails, play areas and wildlife reserves. A café is being created from the nineteenth-century coal store, and this will have panoramic views of the wetlands. The creation of the wetlands requires a fair deal of hard work and expertise. Reeds are being transplanted and new waterways dug, lined with hazel and chestnut sticks, and silt is being dredged from lakes and transferred to shallower ponds. Deep channels – urban bayous – are being dug to manage reed growth and protect ground nests from foxes. The wetlands are already being populated by more and more birds, such as herons and kingfishers.

Local young adults will be employed as rangers to enforce basic rules (such as no dogs) to prevent the disturbance of the wildlife and to give the local community a sense of ownership and pride. Crucially, wildlife will live alongside people, with the wetlands freely open to the public. A primary school is being built along one reservoir, which will provide many children with their first encounter with wildlife and reverse their Nature Deficit Disorder. It is hoped that the mental health benefits, in addition to improved attention and learning, should become apparent.

The desire of people to live by water is exemplified by the fast-rising property prices in nearby Walthamstow village. Ultra-modern towers will soon loom over an area resembling the Norfolk Broads. In Cork, Ireland, the city council has agreed a similar scheme to revitalise its old Docklands by creating a series of urban water gardens and wetlands. In addition to providing a restorative environment for city dwellers, these schemes help to manage rainfall. As global warming causes more evaporation, the air holds more water, and flooding is becoming more commonplace. As this trend continues, the management of rainfall will be one of the most important challenges for city living in the twenty-first century. The Victorian solution to rainfall was focused on getting rid of as much water out of the city as possible, through large pipes or hidden rivers, redirected or merged with sewers. But these drainage systems are increasingly overloaded, not just because episodes of excessive rainfall are increasing, but because we have progressively concreted over our green spaces, leaving nowhere for the water to go. The opening up of covered rivers and canals and creating new wetlands contributes to better rainwater management. However, more ambitious plans include the development of amphibious houses and floodable public squares.

## Floating neighbourhoods

When coastal cities need to expand, one solution now commonly being explored is to build on the water. The Netherlands, a densely populated coastal country, has a head-start when it comes to building floating homes. One-third of the country lies below sea level, so its planners, architects and engineers have become expert at holding back the tides with dykes, dams and floodgates. The lakes that have been created provide opportunities for housing expansion.

The Dutch recently built a whole floating neighbourhood on Lake IJmeer, east of Amsterdam (see opposite). The largest floating community in the world, it contains 158 three-storey townhouses and some high-rise towers, all arranged around canals or floating boulevards, complete with floating schools, bars, restaurants and churches. The buildings's concrete hulls act as passive temperature regulators – the water warming the homes in winter and cooling them in the summer. And unlike homes built on land, these are entirely moveable: disconnect them from the jetties supplying their water, energy and drainage, and they can be moved around, to be plugged in somewhere else.

Floating houses, Lake IJmeer, Holland

Besides the pragmatic motives in favour of living on the water, another, more aesthetic argument is that it fosters a feeling of liberty and of closeness to nature.

## Urban beaches

Urban beaches are another way of accessing water's restorative power, even if only temporarily. Temporary beaches are created every summer along the South Bank of the Thames in London, along the Seine in Paris, and in Stockholm, Copenhagen and Berlin. Swimming is not possible in most cases, but simply being next to the water, as well as the emotional cues of a permanent beach, can make the experience almost as restorative.

If you live in Sydney, there are real beaches on your doorstep, but the beach precincts are mostly unfrequented by the inhabitants of this sprawling and often congested city. Researchers have found that the key to enticing a Sydneysider onto the beach is to improve its access and walkability. This inevitably makes it feel more open, inviting and safe – all features of any public space that make us want to use it.

## Nature + exercise = maximum happiness

Exercise has a beneficial effect on mood, whatever the environment. However, we are increasingly aware that if exercise happens in blue or green space the positive effect is increased. The optimal benefit comes from group sports, compared with solo running, although both are very beneficial. The former has the tendency to encourage more vigorous exercise by stealth and has the added bonus of increased social contact. The health-giving effects of exercise in a park might result from the *synergy* of sensory stimulation and physical exercise.

The Green Gym project run by the European Centre for Environment & Human Health (ECEHH) encouraged people to exercise in green spaces rather than in a gym. The effects on well-being were dramatic. A systematic review of similar research (including information on 833 adults over 11 trials) vindicated their finding. Most trials showed an improvement in mental wellbeing: compared with exercising indoors, exercising in natural environments was associated with greater feelings of revitalisation, increased energy and positive engagement, together with decreases in tension, confusion, anger and depression. Participants also reported greater enjoyment and satisfaction with outdoor activity and stated that they were more likely to repeat the activity at a later date. This last point is particularly interesting, because long-term health outcomes are more likely to be influenced by persistent changes in lifestyle. Future research needs to follow people up over time, and explore the effect of natural environments on sticking to exercise.

There is also a Blue Gym project, exploring the benefits of swimming, surfing, kayaking and so on, or of simply jogging along the coast, with promising early results. In a heartwarming study of war veterans with post-traumatic stress disorder (PTSD), surfing helped to ease their symptoms and reinvigorated their sense of camaraderie. The positive effects lasted beyond the surfing session itself.

Returning to green spaces, local councils can help to facilitate the use of parks and commons for exercise in the city. In recent years the number of local residents carving out running tracks around Clapham Common in south London has increased dramatically. Lambeth Council, working together with the Clapham Common Trust, has provided water fountains for the runners. Small gestures like this make a park feel like part of the community, adapting to its needs. Good public spaces do not just happen by accident. The best ones are carefully planned to maximise our engagement with exercise, other people and wildlife.

Chapter 16

# Recreational buildings

It was an incidental finding of research on viewing natural scenes that we preferred pictures with people in them. While open spaces might bring people together, it is the recreational building that has the most potential for encouraging casual social contact, and making friends.

## Sociopetal and sociofugal forces

Recreational buildings should be open and welcoming, and once we are inside they should encourage us to interact: the design of their interiors orients the occupants toward each other. Spaces that do this are 'sociopetal'. Internal spaces that deter eye contact (which signals our intention to interact) are 'sociofugal'. These terms are borrowed from the physical forces experienced in angular motion. On a waltzer or carousel, as the speed picks up, we feel a strong force pushing us outwards – away from the ride, and other people. In contrast, a satellite orbiting the Earth has a centripetal force acting on it – it is pulled in towards the Earth by the force of gravity. It is only its velocity that keeps it from spiralling inwards. So, in sociology, sociofugal forces push us apart, while sociopetal forces bring us together. Sociofugal forces are antisocial, leading to alienation. Sociopetal forces are prosocial.

In some public buildings, a sociofugal effect is wanted – like in a doctor's waiting room. Here we feel vulnerable and want more privacy. Open-plan offices, or hospital wards, where lines of sight are blocked by walls or screens, are also sociofugal. However, a recreational building should not be sociofugal – this is, simply, bad design. Even so, there are limits to how much buildings should encourage social contact. Not all of us are comfortable with very sociopetal buildings. Perhaps not surprisingly, a study conducted by Benjamin Meagher and Kerry Marsh, at the University of Connecticut, found that extroverts preferred more prosocial layouts. Agreeableness (reflecting a strong desire to please others) was also predictive of a preference for prosocial layouts. However, introverts preferred sociofugal ones. Meagher and Marsh also studied another factor influencing our attraction to sociopetal spaces: our prevailing feeling of inclusion or exclusion in the lives of our peers. Research has shown that individuals who feel temporarily excluded from a social group generally strive to reconnect with the social group, and scan for opportunities to do so. However, when there is no obvious opportunity to re-engage socially, they withdraw, increasingly fearful of rejection. In this state of alienation, they flee from prosocial spaces, preferring more private ones.

Meagher and Marsh carried out a series of experiments which proved this. They designed some online tasks which were intended to ensure that certain individuals were ostracised. In the first experiment the participant wrote an introduction about themselves (a character description) to other members of a (fake) online community of eleven people. Everyone was then at liberty to 'like' each other's descriptions. The community was rigged so that everyone apart from the ostracised participant received between two and seven likes. The ostracised victim received just one like. In another experiment – an online pass-the-ball game – the participant was included at first but quickly excluded, with the other players just passing the ball among themselves. The result of these cruel experiments was that the ostracised participants expressed a preference for a centrifugal room layout over a centripetal one.

When designing social spaces, designers need to be aware that people do not like to be positioned so that they are directly facing one another. For example, being forced to sit or stand face to face with someone is less conducive to social interaction than being offset at an angle. In fact, facing someone square on is often perceived as oppositional and intimidating. 'Squaring up' can signal imminent aggression, and can trigger a fight-or-flight response. Boxers square up to promote a match. Competitors are face-on in a chess game.

For this reason, therapists and psychiatrists are trained never to face their patients directly, while the ideal positioning of professional and client is in a 'ten to two' arrangement. Some of the early observational research on personal space, by the environmental psychologist Professor Robert Sommer, of the University of California, noted that if staff and patients in a hospital cafeteria did not know each other, they preferred to sit at right angles at a table. These observations are all relevant to any recreational building, where social contact is being encouraged. We do not want to be *forced* to communicate. When avoiding social proximity is difficult, this can be a problem. The less we know someone, the more personal space we need between us and them – at least at first.

When a building is overcrowded our personal space is threatened.

Personal space is a concept that only really took off as a research topic in the 1960s. The cultural anthropologist Edward T. Hall was the first to define the study of personal space, or 'proxemics', which he expressed as 'the interrelated observations and theories of man's use of space as a specialized elaboration of culture'. Put more simply, it is the scientific study of the cultural norms of acceptable social distance.

Personal space can be divided into roughly four zones, which in the UK, Europe and the USA could be defined approximately as follows: intimate (0–18 inches/45 centimetres); personal social contact (18 inches to 4 feet/14 centimetres to 1.2 metres); unfamiliar social contact (4–12 feet/1.2–3.6 metres); and public meetings (12–25 feet/3.6–7.6 metres). Famous experiments conducted by Harold Garfinkel at UCLA in the 1960s starkly demonstrated what happens when we deliberately flout these rules of social contact. Researchers were instructed to sit close to someone on a park bench, at a distance that was less than the normal personal space for that setting. Peoples' reactions were strongly aversive – they became bewildered and embarrassed, usually moving on or away from the person intruding on their personal space.

Crowding on public transport is a good example of how personal space is compromised on a daily basis, during the work commute. Various mental techniques are used to cope with the discomfort, such as avoiding eye contact or conversation, and even 'dehumanising' – pretending that the person in close proximity isn't human. Extensive research of underground trains has revealed that as carriage density increases, many of us will opt not to occupy available seats but to stand in places that maximise physical distance from other passengers. When this is no longer possible, as further seats are filled, those sitting use a number of avoidance techniques, with passenger bodies turned towards the sides of the carriage and away from people, with arms crossed.

Researchers at Cornell University authored a study subtitled 'Please don't make me sit in the middle'. They were able to detect spikes in cortisol, the stress hormone, for passengers who were forced to sit in close proximity to others. Interestingly, spikes in cortisol are not seen in response to general overcrowding, but in response to the close proximity of a seated passenger. Personal space is linked to the concept of territory and defensible space.

In fact, personal space is merely a 'portable' version of territoriality. The psychologist Irvin Altman defined three main classes of territory with different levels of permeability. Primary territories are private and restricted to the owner and carefully guarded against intruders. Secondary territories are more open to other people but are still not entirely available to all. And public territories are supposedly self-explanatory but actually quite difficult to define.

The boundary between public and secondary territories is fluid – also, public spaces vary in the degree to which they are public. For example, in London, Clapham Common is more accessible than Hyde Park. Parks are gated, and the gates are closed at dusk. In contrast, commons have no fences or gates. When we settle for a while in a public space we often 'adopt' a space around as a temporary private territory – using what Sommer called 'markers' like shopping bags or papers to stop other people coming too close. Sommer famously observed that people studying in libraries would create artificial barriers between themselves and others with piles of books, coats or bags.

Close proximity to a large number of strangers has been shown to cause stress in most people. It can also cause increased aggressiveness. Slowed-down films of people walking on busy pavements demonstrate how much concentration is required to avoid bodily contact and eye contact. Avoiding the latter seems to be instinctive because eye contact normally indicates intimacy or aggression. An increased density of children in a nursery increases the amount of aggression and verbal expression of bad temper; and the more crowded the prison, the greater the incidence of riots and disturbance among inmates. Public buildings that are too small for their occupants kill conversation.

There are, of course, individual differences in our tolerance of overcrowding. Some individuals are more tolerant of the invasion of personal space, but there are a number of studies that show how if we are in a crowded situation we do less well at cognitively demanding tasks, like arithmetic. We tend to be slower and make more errors. We also feel more anxious as is confirmed by the biological evidence of this – including raised blood pressure and increased pulse rate. However, a subset of people, who score low on personal space demands, can demonstrate *improved* performance in a crowded situation. People scoring high on extroversion tend to find the close proximity of other people more distracting than introverts do when trying to complete difficult attention tasks. Extroverts might claim to be more tolerant of crowded places, and might thrive in them, but they are less able to focus their attention than introverts, who might be more expert at blocking out people around them.

When we are in crowded situations we tend to become more annoyed with others while attempting group tasks, and express anger more readily. This negative effect of crowding on prosocial behaviour can be mitigated to an extent if people can reduce noise interference (perhaps by listening to headphones or by installing acoustic insulation in a building). Providing partitions and increasing illumination can reduce the perception of crowding. The stress of overcrowding is also reduced if we have breakaway spaces. These give us a greater sense of control. If we feel that invasions of personal space cannot be controlled, stress accumulates and leads to a state of passivity and withdrawal (known as learned helplessness). In the case of a public building, people will simply stop using it.

## Semiprivate spaces

Sharing communal facilities, like a café or kiosk, will encourage social contact in a public space, but there is a balance to be struck in terms of the size of the open space around them. The space cannot be too small or too large. There will be an optimum density, and an optimum number of people. It is about having opportunities for pairs of people to spark up a conversation. If a room is too large, it can be subdivided with partitions or have breakaway spaces that are semiprivate.

Technology has allowed architects to create buildings that are much more open. Before the invention of steel-framed buildings and reinforced concrete, more internal walls were needed to keep them standing. The taller and wider the building, the thicker the walls and columns had to be. Now buildings can be designed to let you see right through them, from one side to the other. That means that we can visually connect with others and feel less confined. Of course, having more open public buildings can produce unwanted noise disturbance when we are tasked with a piece of work. But mostly we seem to feel stimulated by human noise when we are at leisure (not at work, as we will see later).

Dr Michal Dębek of the University of Wroclaw carried out a study of five shopping malls in Poland to determine what factors made for a more pleasurable shopping experience. To his surprise, noisy and crowded malls were preferred over calmer ones. The design and layout of the shops themselves, contrary to popular belief, had very little impact on a mall's perceived attractiveness.

It seems that when we are in places of leisure and play we like the buzz of other people – although, as we have discussed, there are limits defined by our personal space. We can tolerate a bit more intrusion than we can in a home or a waiting room. Perhaps this is because we feel more in control. We can escape whenever we want to a calmer, less crowded place. We can dip into busy recreational spaces, taking what we want from them. One important lesson, though, is for public spaces to feel open and permeable. If a place is permeable to the street, it is not only more welcoming, it feels safer, because we have a ready route of escape, especially if there are clear sightlines across the internal space – another important design feature for a public building. We want to be able to understand the limits of the space, and how we enter and exit. We also need those semiprivate spaces designed into the building.

Design affects not just how we can cope with the density of people in a public space, but also how much we enjoy a specific recreational activity within it. For example, the shape of a concert hall might influence how much we enjoy the performance of the orchestra.

## Music venues

Dr Jukka Pätynen and his team, of Aalto University, Finland, used mock-ups of some of the most famous music halls in Europe to test the effect of the different designs on how much emotion the audience felt, including both a subjective measure and a physiological measure of emotional arousal – electrical skin conductance (otherwise known as the galvanic skin response, or the Lie Detector test).

They presented twenty-eight test subjects, aged twenty-two to sixty-four, with a recorded excerpt of Beethoven's Symphony No 7. The experiment was carried out using a surround loudspeaker system in a listening room adapted to mimic the rectangular or non-rectangular concert halls of six European venues, including the Vienna Musikverein, Amsterdam Concertgebouw, Berlin Konzerthaus and Philharmonie, Cologne Philharmonie and Helsinki Music Centre.

The same piece of music was played for each design. During listening, the skin conductance was measured by sensors attached in the listeners' fingers.

The results revealed that the music had a stronger emotional impact when presented in the acoustics of a shoebox-shaped concert hall, such as the Vienna Musikverein or Berlin Konzerthaus. This was consistent with the participants' reported experiences in the halls themselves, with Vienna Musikverein having the most impact on them, followed by Berlin Konzerthaus.

## The Casa da Música

Good public buildings are inviting and bring us together. Unsocial spaces are full of barriers, physical or acoustic. We looked at the Casa da Música in Porto, Portugal, in Chapter 1 in our discussions about how mystery can be overdone. Casa da Música is a concert hall that also attempts to be a place of intrigue and play. The hall itself is surrounded by a rabbit warren of angular rooms and corridors of wildly varying shapes and textures. The architect is Rem Koolhaas, a former screenwriter, who has designed the interior to be like a series of jump cuts in a film: as you travel around the building the materiality and lighting in each room contrast abruptly with the last. There are aluminium floors, rubber walls, and metal grilles, flashes of neon and bits of classic Portuguese tile.

His intention was to cause complexity and intrigue – to fire up our instinctive curiosities – but as we have learnt, complexity needs to exist within some order. I visited the building as a contributor to *The Secret Life of Buildings*, a Channel 4 documentary presented by Tom Dyckhoff. He initially found the place 'weird' but playful. But he and I then interviewed a few of the people who use the building every day. For them, there was *too much* stimulation. They also found navigating the building on a daily basis stressful – a result of the architect's deliberate experiment with disorientation.

After spending several hours in the building, I definitely began to feel a creeping anxiety. When it came to making my final comments to camera, the adjective that leapt in to my brain was *psychotic*.

In other words, it had an incoherent and disorienting quality. As the influential psychiatrist Jaspers would have put it – it was purposefully 'non-understandable' in its disordered references to old and new Porto. It reflects a series of fractured unconnected moments, perhaps expressing the chaos of modern urban life. To Koolhaas, this is realistic. Life is never a series of smooth transitions. Although it is impossible to understand the building, both conceptually and spatially (there are no clear lines of site through it), he would not see that as a problem. The building is about adventure. It is meant to satiate our curiosity for exploration, slowly revealing its myriad awkward-shaped spaces.

The building is a place of shock and awe as opposed to a social space. It is there to entertain us, but we are passive in that experience – it does not really have a lot of meaning to the visitor, and as such they do not playfully interact with it. If Koolhaas had wanted to invite us to play in the building, he failed. It is far too easy to get lost, or to lose each other, and there are not enough views out.

Casa da Música fails as a social space. It has too many narrow twisting corridors and stairs with minimal seating. These corridors serve to separate people, with precious little opportunity for breaking off into pairs in semiprivate spaces. There just isn't room. The building is for show, not for sharing. It feeds our need for curiosity initially but ends up exasperating us.

Interestingly, the angular stone landscaping surrounding the building was much more successful as a play space. Skateboarders were making good use of the smooth ramps and humps (see overleaf). Others huddled in groups with coffees or sandwiches. Meanwhile, the impenetrable café inside was more or less empty.

Inside the Casa da Música, Porto

Skateboarding and socialising outside the Casa da Música

A building that reflects our fractured lives is an interesting artistic statement, but buildings must be more than just statements. They must be livable. As science tells us more about how our buildings affect us, architects should provide an antidote to the atomising effects of capitalism, by creating spaces that pull us closer together. Tourism is a form of play and iconic, sculptural buildings like Frank Gehry's Guggenheim Museum, Bilbao, in

Spain, arguably encourage such play. We mostly admire their exterior, though. Unless the inside matches the splendour of the outside, we do not spend long in them.

The Guggenheim in Bilbao is a sculpture in titanium. It is all about the exterior. A glittering tribute to the city's long-declined shipping industry, it is also a beacon of regeneration, and a thing to be gawped at by multitudes of tourists – a place of play and recreation. Most people come for the building, not the art. Perhaps a minority enjoy the art. However, the interior is less successful than the exterior. This is not a building designed to facilitate play. There is nothing interactive or sociable about it. It is designed from the outside in, leaving the interior confusing and fragmentary, much like the Casa da Música. Visitors tend to spend more time being photographed next to its shining walls, before settling down for a drink or a bite in the traditional squares of the city. Again, the informal open spaces around the building and elsewhere in the city are more successful in getting people together than the formal ones.

The Tate Modern building on London's South Bank is a successful public building for many different reasons. First of all, it is a redesign of a huge Victorian power station, which gives it a sense of history and place. Secondly, it has a large, open entrance and the huge scale of the turbine hall has been preserved, giving clear lines of site across the whole building – visitors can immediately understand its limits and feel a visual connection to other people. Finally, the architects were aware that the building was not just a place to view art, but a social space. In the new extension in particular, there are many breakaway spaces where people can sit and chat.

In general, we prefer the antiquated building to the new. Beijing is more visited than the completely remodelled Shanghai because of its ancient architectural sites. Within Shanghai, it is the old colonial buildings of the Bund which attract. France is the most visited country in the world, perhaps because its towns and villages are well preserved.

The British architectural critic, historian and architect, Professor Kenneth Frampton has expressed despair at how modern architecture has failed to create modern buildings that have the same meaning as a historical building. Instead we resort, in our desperation, to celebrating 'non-place' and kitsch – the bowling alleys, bars and restaurants found in the suburban sprawls of cities like Los Angeles and Las Vegas. Rather than celebrating these 'decorated sheds' of post-modernism, he argues that these places are generating further alienation and loneliness.

The human instinct to form social groups is still very evident in the young populations of our cities. The most unpromising of urban spaces – from abandoned markets to undercrofts, warehouses and bits of wasteland – can become places of cultural significance. These are the junk places where our young creatives organise and get together to create a sense of place. The key to protecting public life is to foster this process, and protect it from developers and franchises.

Franchises impose a symbolic identity on a public building, which is of little interest to psychologists and architects. It is important for most McDonald's restaurants to look the same, in order to communicate that the public knows what they are going to get – it's a safe bet that the hamburger will taste the same as 'back home'. But they are entirely placeless, by design. They could exist anywhere in the world. And they are designed to deter the customer from staying too long – bright lighting and hard seating contribute to that. Real places are developed around an independent local vision – a café and social club developed by and for the local community, an impromptu venue, a local club, a library. Architects can help to foster such localism by using the undeveloped spaces within a city, the spaces between buildings, providing help in the design but not dictating it.

As cultural norms change, recreational buildings will adapt. Community is more complex and ephemeral than a refined box or decorated shed would imply. And messy social and economic realities are reasserting themselves in the recent craze for pop-up bars, restaurants and other social spaces, and through artist studios carved out of disused warehouses. Tough credit-crunch realities have had some positive social consequences by increasing the number of rent-free spaces for people to use to serve their own communities.

Brixton Market, a once failing and dilapidated retail space, has become one big thriving restaurant, with old market lots selling everything from Colombian street food to luxury fried chicken with a side of *pisco* sours. It is vibrant, cosmopolitan and inviting. It has become the beating heart of an area that once saw one of the worst urban riots of modern times.

## Understanding the headspace of public spaces

The best recreational spaces, for children and adults, are natural spaces – green and blue spaces. The best stress-buster is a combination of exercise and natural environment. Recreational buildings are the next-best thing, provided they are designed to be open, permeable and inviting. Depending on the activity, they should be big enough to accommodate the right number of visitors, so that personal space is not threatened. We must embrace our young creatives, who will give recreational buildings a sense of place.

Just as important as play for a happy, well-adjusted life is having a productive working environment. We all need to feel productive. In the next chapter we will explore how design can affect satisfaction, stress levels and performance at work.

Part Six

# The Workplace

Assuming an average forty-hour week, we spend just over one-third of our waking hours at work, while 84 per cent of us work more than our contracted hours (UK data). Over one-third of us never use all of our allocated lunch break, and most of us just eat at our desks. Although remote working is on the rise, we still do most of our work in offices. Given how much time we spend in these often sterile environments, it is important to consider their psychological influence on us. How do the designs of these offices make a difference to our levels of stress and productivity? How should they be laid out? Should they be open-plan, partitioned or enclosed? How should they be lit and decorated? How should they be furnished?

Dr Peter Barrett of Salford University in the UK found that up to 17 per cent of the variance in a child's learning in the classroom could be influenced by simple aspects of design, including indoor air quality, ambient light and whether the space was only moderately stimulating or 'awash in visual clutter'. Similar considerations apply to adults in offices.

# Chapter 17

# Open-plan?

In the last century, the invention of reinforced concrete made it possible to have large open-plan spaces, because structural walls were no longer necessary. This made possible one of the biggest transformations of the workplace over the last half century – the now ubiquitous open-plan office.

Many justifications have been given for working in an open-plan environment. The perceived positives for workers were that this reduced social isolation, and increased interaction and collaboration. Possible advantages for the employer included getting more employees into the same space and having better supervision of the workforce. Also, building an open-plan office is much cheaper than the alternative.

Steve Jobs was reputedly fanatic about the open-plan design at Pixar's headquarters in California, because of its potential for unplanned collaborations. In Facebook's huge Menlo Park headquarters in California, open-plan workstations are the norm. Even Mark Zuckerberg, the company's CEO, sits at the same type of open-plan workstation provided for all employees. He does, however, get the added benefit of a personal conference room. The design team, Gensler, followed the principle of employees having 'easy access to their teams to meet, critique, refine, brainstorm, iterate, and develop'.

However, the team also attempted to find a balance between collaboration and private space, where people could hide away, 'to imagine, muse, write, reflect, create, and just be alone with their thoughts'.

Surveys show that open-plan working is not popular among employees if there is nowhere to go for more focused work. Jungsoo Kim and Richard de Dear, of the Faculty of Architecture at the University of Sydney, found that enclosed offices were generally preferred over open-plan ones. There was a privacy–communication trade-off, which, on balance, favoured privacy: ease of interaction didn't rate as a major concern for office workers compared to avoiding visual and noise disturbance. As we learnt in the studies on student dorms, uncontrolled social interactions and interruptions are distressing. They can cause overstimulation and a reduced ability to focus on the task in hand. Conversely, some researchers have found that having an open-plan office might actually dissuade interaction because conversations are not private, and can disturb others. Neither outcome is desirable.

Lack of visual privacy has a major effect on satisfaction in a completely open-plan office. Not surprisingly, this improves with the addition of partitions, and with the height of partitions. However, lack of sound privacy was a much bigger determinant of worker satisfaction than any other environmental problems. So, the positive effect of improved visual privacy tended to be nullified and even reversed by the problem of noise interference.

Counter-intuitively, offices with high partitions led to *even more* noise interference than a completely open-plan arrangement. The flimsy materials often used to form boundaries in large offices frustrate expectations that noise will be reduced. In reality, when people are out of sight they are out of mind; workers often make *more* noise, have louder conversations and so on if they can't see the effect that it is having on their colleagues. So, the Sydney survey revealed that workspaces with no or limited partitions registered higher satisfaction for 'sound privacy' and 'noise level' than did cubicles with high or low partitions. In summary, the only thing worse than an open-plan office for noise pollution is an office with high-partition cubicles.

Uncontrollable noise doesn't just lower productivity, it also decreases overall motivation. It can come from a number of sources, like the printer, copier, coffee machine and so on, but overhearing irrelevant conversations is the most distracting and demotivating. It is particularly disruptive of complex verbal tasks, like preparing a talk. Headphones are a solution, but are often banned in the workplace. They can give the impression that employees are distracted from their work. They also make it necessary for a colleague to use visual contact prior to initiating a conversation.

As a compromise, many open-plan offices now have buzz rooms where private meetings can take place. For the Interpolis insurance building in Tilburg, Holland, after research into the kinds of work people do, the office spaces were designed accordingly. The majority of time employees to do not sit at their desks – they have both informal and formal meetings with colleagues, research, brainstorm, meet and greet visitors. So, in addition to open-plan spaces, there are a variety of meeting places of varied size and level of privacy. You can choose the working space that best fits the work you have to do –

and in the Tivoli extension, with a variety of workplace installations designed by eight different architects, you can also select the atmosphere you want. These include quirky 'clubhouse' structures.

Google's Tel Aviv headquarters also gets the balance right in the privacy–communication trade-off. According to the designers Camenzind Evolution, 'Nearly 50 per cent of all areas have been allocated to create communication landscapes, giving countless opportunities to employees to collaborate and communicate with others.' This leaves 50 per cent of space for more private, focused work: 'There is clear separation between the employees' traditional desk-based work environment and those communication areas, granting privacy and focus when required for desk based individual working and spaces for collaboration and sharing ideas.'

This fifty–fifty arrangement avoids the tyranny of open-plan offices with no quiet, private area. Inescapable noise doesn't just lead to dissatisfied employees, it also impairs concentration and increases stress and irritation levels. Research has shown that over time the physical symptoms of stress (headaches and fatigue) become apparent and there is an increase in days off work due to illness. It is easy to see why employees in this environment are more likely to be dissatisfied with their jobs, and more critical of their own job performance. It is also easy to comprehend the known effect on reduced productivity. There is no habituation: the problems of the open-plan office do not reduce over time. In other words, employees coming from enclosed offices do not get used to open-plan ones. Levels of mental and physical distress remain high, and productivity relatively low.

Exceptions to this are seen in people with a highly developed ability to screen out unwanted noise in the environment. Alena Maher and Courtney von Hippel, of the School of Psychology, University of New South Wales, Sydney, have shown that people with this high 'inhibitory capacity' did much better on tests of attention and had higher levels of satisfaction and performance in an open-plan setting. Interestingly, individuals with a better ability to block out unwanted noise perceived their workstation as being more private than those without this ability to focus their attention.

### Noise absorbers

In the Google Dublin campus, there is ample use of noise-absorbent material on the ceilings and via indoor plants and soft furnishings.

Research by the Indoor Environment Laboratory in Finland has shown how adding absorbent materials to the ceilings and walls could make a big difference to work performance. The researchers created an office laboratory that was as close to real-world conditions as possible. Background speech was broadcast through four speakers in the corners of the room. Four different conditions were compared:

1. No interventions to reduce noise (reflective surfaces)
2. Sound absorption increased on the ceiling, walls and screens using mineral wool, but without masking noise
3. A masking background noise
4. The quiet condition (no background speech at all)

The participants completed tests of working memory. Questionnaires measured ratings of subjective distraction and disturbance.

Acoustic design had a significant effect on working memory, especially with increasing task difficulty. As expected, individuals performed worse in Condition 1 – the no mask, no absorption condition. Interestingly, performance was even better in Condition 3 than in the quiet condition. Perhaps the sound of other participants tapping on their keyboards was enough to affect performance.

Unsurprisingly, there was a general increase in both disturbance and distraction in individuals identified as 'noise sensitive'. If the individuals were *not* noise sensitive, their perceived disturbance decreased progressively from Condition 1 to 4. However, noise-sensitive people were still experiencing a lot of disturbance in Condition 2. Disturbance was then reduced by a modest amount (30%) in Condition 3, and by about 90% in Condition 4, the quietest. So, people who are sensitive to noise will function optimally only in privately enclosed offices, a luxury not often afforded to employees in the modern workplace.

### Soothing noises

Research has shown that playing soothing sounds at the end of a work shift has some restorative value for stressedd-out open-plan workers. Helena Jahncke and her colleagues, of the Department of Environmental Psychology at the University of Gävle in Sweden, recreated the sound conditions of an open-plan office in a laboratory. After a period of exposure to this noise, individuals who watched a nature video with the noise of a flowing river had increased feelings of vitality compared to those who were exposed to more office noise, or to a mixture of office noise and river sounds. Individuals exposed to noise in the 'restoration phase' also experienced reduced motivation.

## The importance of atmosphere

The quality of lighting in an office is often overlooked, but it has important psychological effects. This is not a niche concern: a survey conducted by the American Society of Interior Design indicated that 68 per cent of employees complain about the lighting situation in their offices. Artificial lighting can be either too dim or too harsh. Until the late 1980s, the US post office in Reno, Nevada suffered from dim and poorly directed lighting. After it was renovated, the illumination was greatly improved. Productivity subsequently increased dramatically – the mail sorters became the most efficient in the western half of the country, with machine operators boasting the lowest error rates.

However, natural light has a much more powerful effect on performance than artificial light, no matter how carefully the latter is designed. There are some companies that recognise the importance of daylight. For example, the designers of the Menlo Park Facebook headquarters have used an extensive system of windows and skylights to ensure that workstations are exposed to the sun's rays.

Access to natural daylight is thought to improve learning because it reinforces the natural sleep-wake cycle (circadian rhythm). According to circadian neuroscientist Russell Foster at the University of Oxford in the UK, natural light contains more blue light than artificial light. So, for example, natural light contains 500 times more blue light than an LED. The blue light photoreceptors in our retinas are tasked with regulating our daily rhythms and evolved separately from vision. They contain a pigment called Opn4, which uses blue light as a signal that the brain should suppress the sleep-inducing hormone melatonin and release brain chemicals that make us more alert.

So, carefully designed buildings, such as Menlo Park, can reverse what Foster called 'our increasing detachment from the sun'. A modern office building stays up because of a concrete or steel frame. The outer walls are merely coverings to keep out the weather, so they can be permeated with as much glass as desired.

Maximising our exposure to sunlight should produce employees who are more engaged, happy and productive. Mirjam Münch, an expert in chronobiology and sleep at the Charité – Universitätsmedizin in Berlin, studied a group of twenty-five volunteers exposed to natural or artificial light over the course of two work days. She demonstrated much greater alertness and a more positive mood towards the end of the day in the group exposed to natural light. In contrast, the other group suffered from flagging performance as the day went on.

Many people experience a post-lunch dip in energy due to a natural dip in cortisol. It is important during this time to be working in brightly lit conditions, and preferably by a source of natural light. A walk outside might help – a good reason for having lunch not in the office but off site.

Most of us who have worked in offices will know that it is not always possible to work by a source of natural light; and, of course, in northern latitudes artificial lighting is required for a good chunk of the day in winter. So, how do we optimise this artificial lighting to improve wellbeing and performance? Now that we have a range of high-intensity LED technologies, in addition to fluorescent lighting, what is the most beneficial artificial light for our psychological health and cognitive performance?

A study by Breanne K. Hawes and colleagues at Tufts University, Massachusetts, compared the psychological effects of fluorescent lighting and three types of LED lighting, ranging from cold to warm. They rigged up the lights in temporary military shelters. Twenty-four volunteers conducted tests of mood and memory tasks under each of the lighting conditions on separate days.

In the 'event planning' task, participants were required to remember four events in a number of different 'mission scenarios' – for example, 'resupply fuel, tow vehicles, take-down roadblock and return to base'. They were later asked to verify the sequences of the events presented – for example, did they tow the vehicles and *then* resupply? The second task tested visual working memory. Participants were given three minutes to memorise a map containing fourteen labelled buildings and five labelled roads. They were then asked about the relative positions of the places.

The results demonstrated increased mood disturbance in the fluoresecent light condition. Participants rated higher levels of depressed mood and fatigue, and lower levels of vitality/vigour. In general, within the LED gradations, the warmer colour was associated with less depression and fatigue. In both the verbal and visual memory tests, the time taken to reach a correct answer was shorter (performance was better) in the LED conditions than in the fluorescent conditions. Also, in the visual memory task, the reaction times got progressively shorter as the warmth of the LED lights increased. After some additional statistical analysis, they found a strong association between changes in mood and memory performance. More depression and fatigue led to longer reaction times.

So, compared to traditional fluorescent lighting, warmer LED appears to support positive mood, extended wakefulness and better performance on cognitive tasks. The implications are clear. A simple way for employers to have a more efficient and happier workforce is to replace fluorescent lights with LEDs, but they should go for the warm LEDs over the more intense white.

Work performance and happiness are determined not just by the warmth of light, but also by the lighting intensity. Georg Hoffmann and colleagues at UMIT (the University for Health Sciences, Medical Informatics and Technology), Austria, examined the effects of lights of increasing brightness (500–1,800 lux) on eleven male volunteers in an office over three days. Increasing light intensity over the three days improved subjective scores of vitality and concentration. Also measured was the urinary breakdown product of melatonin, a hormone which varies with the sleep-wake cycle. There was greater melatonin change between 9 a.m. and 5 p.m. on Day 2 for the group with greater light intensity.

When factory workers in Sweden were able to vary the intensity of brightness of lights over workstations to suit their needs this led to a 4.5 per cent increase in productivity.

Another important feature of both the Facebook and Google offices is the abundant supply of indoor plants, often chosen to create a certain mood, to partition big spaces and to heighten visual interest. The Dublin Google office has a number of rooms which strongly ape nature – with mocked-up trees that have leaves in autumn colours, bark-like walls and an abundant use of synthetic grass.

We know that plants are restorative and can improve attention (you will recall Rachel Kaplan's theory that nature improves attention by reducing stress, see page 198). This could be good news for work performance. Ruth Raanaas and colleagues at the Norwegian University of Life Sciences tested this hypothesis. Participants were randomly assigned to one of two conditions: an office setting with four indoor plants or the same setting without plants. They were asked to recall the final words of five random sentences in the correct order. When first arriving in the offices, the groups did not differ on performance, but after the experiment was complete it was obvious that the plant group had done better, and they did better still after a subsequent rest. In contrast, resting had no effect on the no plant group, who continued to perform less well.

Another way in which indoor plants might improve work performance is through their absorption of carbon dioxide ($CO_2$). Professor Derek Clements-Croome at Reading University showed that children exposed to ventilation systems which recycled internal air as opposed to blowing in fresh air from outside did worse on simple tests of working memory. Internal recycling increased the amount of $CO_2$ in the air.

A study based in a primary school in Aveiro, Portugal, found that average $CO_2$ concentration in the classroom almost halved over a nine-week period after adding five potted plants. These also soaked up gases such as formaldehyde (released by glues in furniture) and particulates (soot from factories and diesel engines).

The architect Stacy Smedley of Jasper, Alberta, Canada, designed the first portable 'living classroom' in 2013, with the help of the schoolchildren. It contained a living wall for growing tomatoes and herbs. This idea is slowly catching on in the office.

The decor of the office spaces in Google Dublin varies from natural (restorative browns and greens) to brightly colourful and stimulating (reds, yellows and orange hues; see below). Stimulating colours might, in moderate amounts, improve work performance. In children, a twelve-point increase in measured IQ has been observed in classrooms painted with bright colours instead of neutral colours.

However, an office-based study published in the *Journal of Color Research and Application* suggests that exposure to too much red colour might increase anxiety over time, and *reduce* work performance. Employees placed in offices with blue, red or white walls (thirty employees in each) were compared. They completed office tasks for four consecutive workdays.

Stimulating colours at Google Dublin

At the end of this time, workers in the red office were more depressed and anxious than individuals in the blue office, who felt positive and relaxed. The results for performance more or less followed the trend for mood.

It got more complicated when an individual's ability to screen out distracting stimuli was taken into account. The high screeners performed better in the red office than in the blue one. Perhaps the alerting effect of the colour red was enough to boost performance without causing too much distress.

The lesson here may be that we must be allowed to take control – moving from workspaces with stimulating colours to areas with natural, restorative colours when we feel overloaded.

In addition to colour, temperature has an important influence over mood and performance. Researchers at Cornell University, in Ithaca, New York state, examined the effects of different office temperatures on employees of a large Florida insurance company. They found that, when the room temperature was lower (20° Celsius), employees made 44 per cent more mistakes than when the temperature was five degrees higher. They speculated that under colder conditions employees were using up a lot of their energy keeping warm, rather than maintaining focus on their work. They also found that when individuals had warmer hands they had greater job satisfaction and felt more generous towards their colleagues.

# Chapter 18

# Self-expression

A striking feature of the Menlo Park headquarters is the opportunity for self-expression. Employees are provided with bare walls on which they are encouraged to make their own art, and write messages to each other. Slogans encouraging individual creativity are to be found everywhere, like 'Fortune favours the bold'.

Giving employees freedom to express themselves can make a big difference to their performance at work in general, and their overall satisfaction. This has been known since the experiments conducted in Chicago's Hawthorne Factory in the 1920s and 1930s (collectively known as the Hawthorne experiments). These showed that individual initiative and varied work improved performance. In one of the most important experiments a number of female workers with a known work rate were placed in a test room, which was separated from the main assembly department by a wooden partition 10 feet (3 metres) tall. The women had no official supervisors (just a research worker observing). They were increasingly encouraged to assume responsibility for their own work and were invited to contribute ideas on how to manage changes to meet demand. Work output increased dramatically compared to that in the main factory – 3,000 electronic products compared to 2,000. Absenteeism was only one-third of that in the main assembly room.

Although other changes were made to their environment – including variations in temperature, humidity and lighting conditions, increased rest breaks, shortened working days and no Saturday working – these changes had less impact than increasing personal initiative. Furthermore, even when conditions were returned to what they had been in the main factory, productivity remained 25 per cent above its original value. Merely showing interest in the opinions of employees is highly motivating.

## The moveable office

A striking example of how design can increase personal control in the work environment is Herman Hertzberger's Centraal Beheer office building in Apeldoorn, Holland. Completed more than four decades ago, it was far ahead of its time and it remains an inspiration to office designers today (see opposite). The sense of ownership is embodied in the moveable office modules that are an integral part of its ambitious design.

The Centraal Beheer is like a Lego building, whose office bricks 'can be added or removed, stacked or filed, according to the needs of the company and its staff'. It is an extraordinary exercise in flexibility that was initially incorporated for commercial reasons – blocks could be added or removed in tandem with fluctuating demand to increase efficiency. However, positive side effects of the modular system are high staff satisfaction and good productivity. A greater feeling of autonomy and control has been shown to have a big impact these outcomes.

Centraal Beheer, Apeldoorn, The Netherlands

Satisfaction is related not only to the ability of staff to expand their workspaces but also to the freedom to customise their appearance. Regardless of office layout, the amount of personal space available for work and storage has been identified as the most important influence over workplace satisfaction, although open-plan offices typically provide less. The worst example of deprivation of personal space is the hot-desking concept, where different colleagues use the same desk at different times, denying any opportunity for personalisation.

The design of the Centraal Baheer is unique in that it creates personal spaces within larger spaces. The modules, 9 metres by 9 metres (30 by 30 feet), are arranged in groups of four, around a central staircase/lift. They have a clear line of sight with other blocks that hang across from them, and those that are above and below. As in Google Tel Aviv, there are informal meeting places (including roof terraces), which are separate from individual departments but are not so clearly demarcated. So, there is a sense of partial privacy and personal control but also a sense of connection to other people in the building.

The ethos of the Baheer was as important as the design in increasing staff satisfaction: staff were encouraged to decorate their workspaces as they wished, grow their own plants and even keep their own pets, including chickens. According to a long-serving manager of the building, rules on pets were made 'slightly stricter' after an employee brought in a cockerel, which caused commotion among the hens.

The building remains an ideal mix between individual freedom of expression and collaboration.


## Understanding the headspace of the work place

Work is an important part of our identity and sense of productivity. We need it for social reasons too. Many people meet their future wives and husbands at work. Most of us work in offices, and how we adapt is important. Some of us are good at screening out noise annoyance, but we can all fail miserably when we are forced to work without some level of privacy, in poor light and in poorly ventilated rooms. As in all other areas in our lives, we crave some access to the natural world, and just as in our homes, we like to be able to stamp some personality on where we work. If we don't address a toxic working environment, we can end up being too ill to work – which brings me to the final chapter.

Part Seven

# Healing Spaces

Health isn't everything, but without health everything is nothing. We rarely think about how hospitals are designed. If we are going to a hospital for investigations or a procedure, it's probably the last thing on our minds. But can good design speed recovery? Can bad design cause stress and delay discharge? Have you ever felt frustrated or unwelcome as a visitor? Did you have a private enough space? How easy was it to navigate? To what extent can we apply what we've learnt in the previous chapters?

In his book *The Architecture of Happiness*, the philosopher Alain de Botton asked this: if our happiness is so shaped by aesthetics, what effect do hospitals have on our healing if we are forced to look at prison-like windows, stained carpet tiles and plastic curtains? Patients are more confident of being looked after well if they are in pleasant, calming environments. Pleasant wards actually improve the relationship between patient and doctor, and help with staff recruitment. Expectations are powerful. If we expect to recover quickly, we often do. Poorly designed or dilapidated buildings produce the opposite: they cause anxiety about recovery, or they dissuade us from seeking help in the first place.

Chapter 19

# A healthy atmosphere

The same themes of light and nature apply to well-designed hospitals as they do to all our other domains of city of life, but what is surprising is how much impact they have on our health.

Impressively light and airy healing spaces are found in Oslo's Akershus Hospital, which was completed in 2008 and won the coveted Better Building Healthcare Award. It is largely built of wood, it is quiet, and patients enjoy views of nature. The dark winters of Norway can have a detrimental effect on the mood of its population, so the hospital prioritises exposure to natural light. According to architect Anne Underhaug, who was involved in designing the hospital, 'Daylight means a lot in Scandinavia because half the year you don't have very much . . . Regulations are very, very strict on daylight. Unlike in the US where you don't have any daylight regulations at all, where you can have an office with no windows . . . Here the operating theatres have windows in as well. Everything, even the X-ray rooms and CT rooms, MRI rooms, all of them have daylight.'

The Sumner Regional Medical Center in Gallatin, Tennessee, has gardens with lush landscaping, tended to by in-house gardeners. Glass walls and floor-to-ceiling windows let in natural light and allow views out. Ulrich's research back in the 1980s compared health outcomes for patients whose beds were next to a window and who enjoyed 'tree views' with those who had only 'wall views'. Patients with tree views had:

1. Shorter hospital stays after surgery
2. A smoother recovery according to nurses
3. A lower use of painkillers
4. A slightly lower frequency of minor post-surgical complications

The Medical University of South Carolina contains a conservatory with glass walls, skylights and indoor plants. This welcomes patients and visitors while serving as the connector between the two main wings of the building. The Bronson Methodist Hospital in Kalamazoo, Michigan created a giant planted atrium in the middle of its hospital building to compensate for the 2 metres (6 ½ feet) of snow that falls in the area each winter, while the sunnier Sharp Memorial Hospital in San Diego has a roof garden. The Saint Rose Dominican Hospitals in Las Vegas have gone one step further by providing gardening classes for their patients in a large indoor garden. Atrium gardens have been shown not only to reduce stress and speed recovery in patients, but also to reduce staff stress, thereby improving the care that they provide.

The Klinik Hirslanden in Zurich has a housekeeping service that tends to the fresh flowers in each room three times a week. This improves comfort and satisfaction, while speeding recovery. Professor Virginia Lohr and colleagues, of the Department of Horticulture and Landscape Architecture, Washington State University, concluded from their studies that indoor plants even increased tolerance to pain: they found that more subjects were willing to keep a hand submerged in ice water for five minutes if they were in a room with plants present than if they were in a room without plants. This was found to be true even when the room without plants had other colourful objects that might help the subject focus on something other than the discomfort. So, the effect was specific to the presence of a natural object, not just visual interest.

From countless studies of pain, we know that stress and anxiety reduce pain tolerance. We also know that a natural environment can buffer against stress, so plants would be likely increase a patient's pain tolerance through this mechanism.

Researchers at the Faculty of Social and Behavioural Sciences at the University of Amsterdam in The Netherlands found that participants were less 'tense', 'uptight' and 'worried' when looking at a ward with plants compared with one without. The researchers also found that green walls reduced stress and speeded recovery compared with white walls. Warm, earthy colours are also thought to be soothing, as provided in the UPMC Hamot Women's Hospital in Pennsylvania, and in the Legacy Salmon Creek Hospital in Vancouver, Canada by the use of wood floors, stone and brick.

If indoor plants are impractical, and there are no views out and no gardens to enjoy, pictures of nature might help. In an acute psychiatric ward in the US, researchers measured the effects of hanging landscape paintings on the bare walls. The number of sedative injections required to calm agitated patients reduced by 70 per cent.

The effect of stress on recovery seems to happen at a cellular level: stress compromises the function of our white blood cells, reducing our ability to fight off infections, and heal. It follows that a calming environment will lead to faster recovery from illness. This also extends to mental illness. Depression, for example, is increasingly understood as an inflammatory reaction to stress. Any reduction in the stress hormone cortisol should speed recovery in addition to the effect of antidepressants.

## Connecting people

Before designing a new neonatal unit for premature babies in Karolinska University Hospital in Sweden, the architect Peter Fröst interviewed parents and care teams about their experiences on the existing unit. Traditionally, mother and baby had recovered on separate wards, which prevented coupling of mother and baby (mothers should hold babies close to their skin as soon as possible after birth). Existing rooms had not been large enough to accommodate infants, mothers and the equipment they both needed to recover. The new combined care unit allowed both mother and baby to recover in the same space. The hospital reported that length of stay was ten days shorter for the most premature infants, rates of illness were lower, fewer infants required ventilator assistance, and the prognosis for physical and mental health over the longer term was improved.

The psychologist Dr Mike Osborn was a consultant in the designing of the award-winning Dyson Centre for Neonatal Care at the Royal United Hospital in Bath, England. This was funded by Sir John Dyson, inventor of the cyclonic vacuum cleaner.

Early sketches for the design showed arms around a baby, as if the building provided a big hug. The aim was to provide a 'secure base', a concept central to Bowlby's attachment theory of child development. Inconsistent care leads to insecure, anxious children and adults. The Dyson Centre gives a feeling of calm solidity. According to Osborn, the centre avoids the hyper-arousing state created by the traditional hospital with its low ceilings, glaring artificial light and lack of privacy.

The psychologist Lucy Maddox studied the building for the Mosaic website. She was impressed by how light and airy it felt. The corridor ceilings were high, with generous skylights giving views to blue sky. The colours were greens and warm beiges, and materials included white-washed wood. Levels of openness and privacy were in a gradation, as the neonates developed into stronger, bigger babies, and the level of clinical intervention became less intense.

The rooms were of generous size, to accommodate families and other visitors, with comfortable, moveable furniture of different heights – higher for peering into an incubator, and lower for sitting with the baby. As Maddox points out 'For a building to be therapeutic, it should have spaces that flex to allow both sociability and privacy. Social spaces with comfortable, movable furniture encourage people to speak to other patients. Places that encourage family and friends to visit, like single-bed rooms or private areas which can be screened off, increase visiting, reduce patient stress and speed up recovery.' The centre manages to get the balance right between sociability and privacy by designing in some flexibility.

With the help of staff at the centre, Dyson's research has been able to prove that the building does actually improve outcomes for the babies compared to the hospital that it replaced. It has shown that the hospital 'is a treatment in itself'.

Professor Mark Tooley, a consultant clinical scientist, led up the team. The health and progress of babies cared for in the old and new hospitals was compared using a number of measures. These included motion sensors (accelerometers) attached to the babies' nappies. Adapted sensors were also used to measure the breathing patterns from the movements of their chest walls. The results showed that the babies in the new centre slept for twenty per cent longer than those in the old unit. According to Dr Bernie Marden, a consultant neonatologist who co-led the research, sleep is crucial for premature babies, because this is when most brain development is done. This impressive result is likely to be due to the direct effect of the more soothing environment on the neonates, but also the indirect effects of more contact from parents and staff.

Researchers used Wi-Fi and infrared receivers to track the movement of staff in the care of ten families in the old building and ten families in the new building. It demonstrated that staff had spent nearly twice as much time in clinical rooms with the babies in the new hospital, when compared to the behaviour of staff in the old unit. The researchers were also able to show that families visited for thirty minutes more each day, and that more mothers breastfed in the new hospital (90 per cent) than in the old one (64 per cent). It is likely that the more inviting and flexible environment made mothers feel more comfortable with breastfeeding their children.

Accommodating visitors is an important part of healing in general. For example, the well-regarded Medical University of South Carolina has pull-out couches for family and visitors included in private patient rooms.

The University of Pittsburgh Medical Center in Pennsylvania found that patient satisfaction and health were enhanced by easily navigable corridors and a better view of patients from them. Laurie Placinski, interior project designer at Progressive AE, Grand Rapids, Michigan, has shown how encouraging patients to move beyond their bedrooms has a 'potential impact on length of stay, as well as decreasing the potential for readmission.' If 'bump zones' are designed into wards (by using circular layouts as opposed to long corridors), these give patients and staff more chance for opportunistic meetings. This social contact boosts a patient's mood and speeds recovery.

It follows that hospitals need to give consideration to wayfinding, for both patients and staff. The psychologist Lucy Maddox explains that having clear signposting in a hospital is important for reducing stress levels in patients and their families. It is also important to reduce wasted clinician time. 'One study in a 600-bed hospital estimated that poor wayfaring cost over $220,000 a year. Much of this was due to the 4,500 hours of clinical time a year – approximately two full-time positions – that was spent giving directions to lost patients and even staff.'

As the elderly population of our cities increases, the designs of our hospitals must be tailored to this age group. The New York Presbyterian Hospital uses sound-absorbing materials to baffle the noise in corridors – crucial for the hard-of-hearing. Clear contrasting colours on walls and floors assist navigation in people with failing sight, as does the use of indirect lighting to reduce glare. The floors are covered with a non-slip material. These design elements get the elderly patients up and moving around the hospital earlier than they would otherwise do.

The hospital is a good example of what can be done to create a place of peaceful recuperation for our elderly.

In addition, walkways should be provided with breakaway semiprivate spaces serving as resting points for elderly patients, while also encouraging some social behaviour. As we learnt in the chapter on public places, these semiprivate spots allow people to pair off and chat. In the Oslo's Akershus Hospital a 'central street' of shops and cafés runs through its large atrium, allowing for normal social activity, and with flexible, more private spaces spinning off it. The design leads to high levels of satisfaction among patients and staff, and despite the fact that it serves a more elderly population than the hospital it replaces, it can still claim shorter hospital stays.

### Single rooms, and a better night's sleep

The best hospitals, like the Akershus Hospital, provide single patient rooms with a window. These result in ten per cent shorter hospital stays than shared bays. This could be explained, in part, by reduced noise disturbance, and therefore improved sleep. It is known that poor sleep impairs the function of the immune system, making it harder to heal and fight off infection. Research has shown that a quieter environment during recuperation in hospital leads to fewer patients being readmitted to hospital after discharge. Not only are single rooms better insulated from the noise of the ward, they are free of artificial light pollution. The natural daylight from the window can help to reinforce our natural diurnal rhythm, improving the quality of sleep and encouraging recuperation. Improved health outcomes might also be due to increased visual checks by nurses. In Florida, patients admitted to an orthopaedic unit for surgery were compared before and after being moved to a new surgical unit with more private rooms. Nurses tended to visit the patients more often after the move, because they had less direct visual contact from the corridor.

## Mental healing

The Therapeutic Garden for the Child and Adolescent Development Institute in Wellesley, Massachusetts was an integral part of the treatment of traumatised children with behavioural disorders.

Its design echoed much of what we have learnt about the balance between security, curiosity and visual interest. Barbara Crisp, author of *Human Spaces*, describes the functions of different parts of the garden: 'The topography of the site was reshaped into a series of archetypal land forms carved by water: a cave-like ravine for safety and security, an upland wooded plateau for exploration, a mount for climbing, an island for seclusion, a pond for discovery, steep and shallow slopes that invite risk, and a large open glade for running and playing.'

The rehabilitation of individuals with severe mental health problems is increasingly set in supported accommodation within the community. Elizabeth Marcheschi at the Lund University, Sweden examined the effects of the physical and social environment in supportive housing for the severely mentally ill. Good examples felt like a home, not a placement. Residents had their say in how they could furnish their rooms, and how the common areas, including the garden, should look. This translated into an increased sense of belonging and emotional attachment to the accommodation, and this in turn increased their emotional and physical wellbeing.

Physical aspects were also important in getting the balance right between privacy and sociability. Through the careful arrangement of furniture in communal areas and smaller, more private areas, social interactions were facilitated, while solitude and restoration was available when needed.

Chapter 20

# End of life

The default option a hundred years ago was to die at home, usually quickly due to infection. Following the discovery of antibiotics, we now tend to die later, most commonly of heart disease or cancer.

Life expectancy doubled over the twentieth century, and as a result our approach to dying changed dramatically. The focus switched from preparation for death to an expectation of a long life. Because technologies like the X-ray machine were so big and expensive, the cottage hospital was replaced by the big centralised hospitals of modern day.

There is a good chance that we will spend our twilight years sitting in rows of chairs, in drab care homes, hospitals or hospices with fluorescent lighting. Many of these places have developed a deservedly bad reputation for their architecture. They are functional, utilitarian places, but the architect Alison Killing argues that hospitals were not always like this. She cites the fifteenth-century Italian Ospedale degli Innocenti, or Hospital of the Innocents, designed by the architect Filippo Brunelleschi. This was a hospital for the dispossessed. The rooms are big with high ceilings, the building is aesthetically beautiful, and large courtyards provide light and air.

Where we die is an important part of how we die, and in this architects can make a difference. For example, Frank Gehry was commissioned to design a cancer care unit in Dundee, Scotland. He confessed to feeling guilty about the issue of whether the extra money spent on his fees could have been put towards more cancer drugs, but good design can be an important part of dying comfortably.

His building forms part of a global chain of Maggie's Centres, hospices named after the late Maggie Keswick Jencks, a former student of architecture who succumbed to cancer in 1995. Maggie was told that she had cancer by a consultant at the end of a twenty-minute appointment. He apologised for having to go to another patient and left her in a hospital corridor, with nowhere to sit, to absorb the news. Maggie's desire to have a more humane space to deal with her illness kick-started an impressive legacy of award-winning hospices. Built on a human scale, they afford calm, privacy and dignity, and each is designed by an accomplished architect – Frank Gehry, Richard Rogers, Zaha Hadid and Daniel Libeskind have each been involved. The centres create a friendlier place in which to personally deal with the disease.

Gehry, a friend of Maggie's, explained: 'I wanted to create a building that would be calming and accommodating, and one that would be a fitting tribute to Maggie. I think it's an inviting building, I think people will want to come inside and spend time there, and I really hope that in some small way it might contribute to a sense of rejuvenated vigor for moving forward and living life.'

Lucy Maddox gave a vivid account of her visit to the Maggie's Centre at Newcastle. She likened it to a Teletubby building:

> . . . surrounded by wild flowers and vibrant green grasses, it is topped off, mushroom-like, with a flattened solar panel. Inside, the building exudes a heavy feeling of calm, like a very expensive, modern house. The building faces south and light floods in through the windows. You can see flowers or grass from every room. Nature is reflected on the inside too, where most of the surfaces are wood. In the kitchen, there's a long wooden table in front of the doors that lead out to the garden. Outside, people are sitting at another table, chatting and drinking tea out of nice mugs. There is nothing clinical about this space. It feels more like somewhere you'd spend a weekend away in the country.

Maddox also describes how it meets the need for mystery: 'areas reveal themselves to you as you explore, like the mezzanine and roof garden that you see only when you walk up the stairs. There are communal, social spaces, and there are little corners where you can curl up and hide away.'

According to one of the architects involved in its design, Lucy Brittain, of the Cullinan Studio, London, it is lots of different types of building in one. 'It's a bit more than a house, but it's not a house, and it's into art, but it's not an art gallery, and it's kind of spiritual, but it's not a church, and it's like a hospital, but it's not medical.' And, because it is all these things and none, it is a beautiful space to adapt to the process of dying; it is a nicer place to be when receiving repetitive, routine chemo or radiotherapy treatments. When there is a lot of hanging around, a stimulating and natural environment becomes more important.

## Maggie's Centre

In 2013, Gehry built Maggie's Centre Hong Kong, the first Maggie's Centre to be built outside the UK. Its rooms and terraces overlook a pond and gardens. The centre offers free support for anyone living with cancer, including friends, family and carers. Visitors can take part in relaxation sessions, nutrition classes, yoga and individual and family support sessions. According to *Dezeen* magazine, 'The Centre's design is a series of pavilions arranged to encourage movement between the interior and the landscape. Rooms open out to the surrounding gardens or have private terraces overlooking the pond. There is a public living and dining area that serves as the focal point of the building, with views of both the ponds and gardens.'

Gehry himself was dealing with death at the time that he was designing the centre, having lost his daughter. His aim was to design something that was 'soothing and respectful' and which offered a way out of the hopelessness of cancer. Users of the centre feel safe, inspired and valued, even when facing their final days.

All over the world, but particularly in developed countries, we are living longer and longer. The proportion of people over 60 years old is predicted to double to 22 per cent by 2050. Perhaps this is why we are so bad at planning for end-of-life care, kicking it down the road. Cultural norms in many Western cultures also exacerbate the problem, dictating still that we avoid talking about death and dying. Hospice care is perhaps the last part of the health care system to get proper attention. It is often impersonal, under-resourced and understaffed, insensitive to the needs of patients, families and the staff. Hospice staff are often paid very low wages, which does not necessarily attract the most highly trained and motivated carers.

Maggie's Centre, Dundee

The design consultancy Fuelfor, based in Singapore and Barcelona, spent nine months researching hospice care and its issues in Singapore. They determined that it was an 'invisible and avoided service'. The work was commissioned by the charitable Lien Foundation and a funeral service foundation. The consultancy came up with a Hospitable Hospice handbook to guide better design, in both look and function. These main principles stood out:

1. Provide an intimate personal care service
2. Avoid the institutional
3. Provide spaces that adapt to the user and normal life

4. Make socialising easy
5. Support the effortless withdrawal to privacy
6. Be open to the wider public
7. Design with family in mind
8. Integrate with nature
9. Make it feel safe

From these general principles emerged their prototype design for the optimal hospice building. It is organised on varying levels of privacy and clinical care, with all the intensive clinical activity occurring on one side of the building. Open to the public, it's intended to give people of all ages, healthy or not, a reason to engage with the hospice facility. The upper floors of the building are more private, with bedrooms and dining for patients, while the lower floors offer green space and tables for the public and patients. Each floor has places to socialise, and places for solitary relaxation.

The ideal hospice does not stop at the threshold. The proposed Open Hospice service in Singapore would provide a food delivery service, a bus service, a spa, a shared garden with a kindergarten and a cinema. These ideas might seem ambitious, but if we plan for end of life earlier (and commit to investing real cash) they might become a reality.

## Understanding the headspace of healing

Nature and loved ones have the power to heal. Ultimately, the extent to which designs for different health care centres provide for access to these determines their success or failure. Access to daylight and gardens, as well as having enough room for visitors, are key. There is also a need for privacy and quiet in your own ward room, and space for you to personalise it, while allowing for navigation into more public areas, with semiprivate breakaway areas for chatting. These are the ingredients for a good quality of life wherever you are in the city, and healing spaces should be no different.

# The ideal city

*I walk down a street lined with trees and I can smell the scents of honeysuckle and rosemary in the small garden we tend to in the square. It's right next to the After Work Club and the local coffee shop. The kids in their school uniforms scamper past the old-timers doing the trip to the local café. I turn down a few residential streets of terraced houses and low-rise apartments before I get to the main street. The traffic is not so heavy since we put in the traffic-calming measures, and we've got a hedgerow planted between the pavement and the road. This soaks up the noise and the pollution. All of human life is here because there are a huge range of rental values, offering up cheap space for micro-businesses, while unused spaces free of rent have been given over to young pop-up businesses. Market stalls are setting up. Cafés are setting out their chairs. It's organised chaos. I say my usual Bonjourno to Ivan. He does the best coffee in the area. I ask him for the usual. I'm on my way to the park for a jog around the lake before work. I pass by the school, with its large adventure playground, partially hidden by trees. The kids are filing through the entrance lobby. There's a library that has become multi-purpose. There's no need to travel across town for yoga, dance classes, car boot sales and cookery courses. This is my home, my neighbourhood and my city. I own it and I love it.*

## Now let's get real

Many of us feel stressed and alienated in the big city. In this context, where we call home is increasingly important. When choice is removed an emotional connection to home is more difficult. For optimal happiness, homes need to meet our basic human needs for refuge, intimacy, expression of identity, and providing hospitality. Do we pay enough attention to (unashamedly) displaying our unique biographies, while at the same time finding space for visitors? Can we add some living things, and perhaps natural colours?

If we have some choice over where we live, should we opt for a home that inspires and stimulates us in its very fabric? If so, it should have tall ceilings and tall windows, a textured, complex façade, a layout with some mystery, and a balance between refuge and openness that suits our personalities. Or are we just at the mercy of government and developers?

Is it even possible to choose a home that feels more connected to the community – a neighbourhood that feels safe (defensible), and that gives us a walkshed life and which is close to a park and a main street and most things that we need to make us content. And if we do live near a main street, can we reclaim it from the traffic? Should we all play a part in producing richly hued streetscapes and buildings that are energised by the fractal patterns of nature? Should we take more control over the greening of our cities – reclaiming unused spaces for parks, gardens and allotments, planting trees and creating planting strips between road and pavement? Gardening is a potent antidote to stress and psychological problems (mediated by physical exercise, the restorative power of nature, and improved self esteem).

As cities grow, these are the questions posed by architectural psychology in the twenty-first century. There are opportunities to get our hands dirty, to shape the development and preservation of our homes, streets and neighbourhoods, to feel a strong sense of ownership, and to build stronger ties with others. The power of social media increases our influence over designing the fabric of our cities. It provides a direct dialogue with architects and planners who are constantly proposing new buildings and schemes – before the first brick is laid. Through its viral sharing of images, it is more iterative and influential than any public meeting. We can even cut out the middle man altogether by crowdfunding the development of new community projects. We know what we want even if we don't often articulate it. For example, public buildings should feel open and inviting, with clear lines of view and breakaway spaces that encourage conversation and play.

When we are sick, the best hospitals and hospices provide us with ubiquitous access to natural light, green views and a perfect balance between peaceful solitude, semiprivate and public spaces.

The secret psychology of our built environment really does matter, and we can find restoration even in the busiest of cities. All we need to do is find a compromise between adapting, harnessing our power for change and prioritising what matters. Ultimately the key to combating stress in the city is remembering what makes us human, dating back to our ancestral pasts. We are social mammals, psychologically adapted to live in groups, to hunt and forage in nature. The history of the city is a baby step in the long journey of humanity's evolution. This book is an attempt to show that cities must bring us together and feed our nature-starved souls.

## Endnotes

**Introduction: The psychology of the city**

Page 9: 'I disagree. People can inhabit anything.' *See:* Heron, Katrina. 'From Bauhaus to Koolhaas', *Wired*, 7 January 1996.

Page 10: '. . . architectural "murder".' *See:* 'Doubt and Reassessment', *Architecture at the Crossroads*, BBC, 1986. BBC Architecture Collection, available on iPlayer. The programme looks at young architects reacting against modernist sterility.

Page 11: 'He did not always blame the architects involved . . .' Ibid.

Page 11: 'International Style.' The *Congrès internationaux d'architecture moderne* (CIAM), or International Congresses of Modern Architecture, was an organisation founded in 1928 with the aim of finding a consensus among the esteemed architects of the age for building housing that met the demands of the modern age. At the fourth conference, in 1933, the scope expanded to urban planning, with the noble aim of solving the increasing problems of overcrowding and squalor in the inner cities – to develop the so-called 'Functional City'. This included separating residential and industrial areas, and moving the population from what were considered slums into tall apartment blocks at widely spaced intervals. The conference proceedings went unpublished until 1943, when Le Corbusier edited them to produce CIAM's 'Athens Charter'. After the Second World War the ideas seemed ever more prescient, and their model for the functional high-rise became known as the International Style. By definition, this was a prototype for housing that had no respect for local context.

Page 12: "'Architecture can't just be about ego . . .'" For Janet Street-Porter's introduction, *see:* http://www.bbc.co.uk/programmes/articles/1mKgxdw0z8zsKwBZvHXVlPg/janet-street-porter-introduces-the-post-war-architecture-collection

Page 12: "'The architect is powerless in isolation.'" *See:* 'Houses Fit for People', *Architecture at the Crossroads*, BBC, 1986. Part of the BBC4 archive, available on iPlayer.

## Part One: The Home, from Inside Out

Page 19: 'Judith Sixsmith . . .' *See:* Sixsmith, J. 'The meaning of home: An exploratory study of environmental experience', *Journal of Environmental Psychology* 6, 1986, pp. 281–298.

## Chapter 1: Refuge versus prospect

Page 23: 'In chapter thirteen of her memoirs . . .' *See:* Barry, Joseph A. 'Report on the American Battle Between Good and Bad Modern Houses', in 1953.

Page 25: 'Kevin McCloud: Most Grand Designs are too big and too bright.' Interview with Sarah Lonsdale. Telegraph.co.uk. *See also* Heerwagen, Judith H., and Gordon H. Orians. 'Humans, Habitats.' *The biophilia hypothesis* (1995).

Page 27: 'It was researchers based . . .' *See:* Alkhresheh, M.M. 'Preference for void-to-solid ratio in residential facades', *Journal of Environmental Psychology* 32, 2012, pp. 234–245.

## Chapter 2: Mystery and complexity

Page 31: 'Research by the American geographer Roger Ulrich . . .' *See:* Ulrich, R.S. 'Visual landscape preference: A model and application', *Man-Environment Systems* 7, 1977, pp. 279–293.

*See also:* Ulrich, R. S. 'Visual landscapes and psychological well-being', *Landscape Research* (England) 4(1), 1979, pp. 17–23.

Page 33: 'Paul Pennartz . . .' *See:* Pennartz, Paul J.J. 'Atmosphere at home: A qualitative approach', *Journal of Environmental Psychology* 6 (2), June 1986, pp. 135–153.

Page 35: 'A study by the environmental psychologist Carolyn Tennessen...' *See:* Tennessen, Carolyn M. and Bernadine Cimprich. 'Views to nature: Effects on attention', *Journal of Environmental Psychology*, 15 (1), March 1995, pp. 77–85.

Page 36: 'The environmental psychologist Rachel Kaplan...' *See:* Kaplan, R. 'Some psychological benefits of gardening', *Environment and Behavior* 5, 1973, pp. 145–152.

Page 37: 'Research by Arthur Stamps...' *See:* Stamps, Arthur E. 'Physical determinants of preferences for residential facades', *Environment and Behaviour* 31 (6), November 1999, pp. 723–51.

Page 39: 'The idea that we can become overwhelmed...' *See:* Akalin, Aysu, Kemal Yildirim, Christopher Wilson and Onder Kilicoglu. 'Architecture and engineering students' evaluations of house façades: Preference, complexity and impressiveness', *Journal of Environmental Psychology* 29 (1), March 2009, pp. 124–32.

## Chapter 3: Closure

Page 50: 'When comparing the landscape preferences...' *See:* Herzog, Thomas R., et al. 'Cultural and developmental comparisons of landscape perceptions and preferences.' *Environment and Behavior* 32 (3), 2000, pp. 323–346.

Page 50: 'A survey, also based in Finland...' *See:* Neuvomen, M. and T. Sievänen, S. Tönnes and T. Koskela. 'Access to green areas and the frequency of visits – a case study in Helsinki', *Urban Forestry and Urban Greening*, 6, 2007, pp. 235–37.

## Chapter 4: Nature in the home

Page 56: 'An alternative explanation, building on Rachel Kaplan's work...' *See:* Kaplan, R. 'The restorative benefits of nature: toward an integrative framework', *Journal of Environmental Psychology* 15, 1995, pp. 169–82.

Page 59: 'Dr Pamela M. Pallett of the Department of Psychology...' *See:* Pallett, Pamela M., Stephen Linka and Kang Leea. 'New "golden" ratios for facial beauty', *Vision Research* 50 (2), 25 January 2010, pp. 149–154.

Page 62: 'According to work conducted by Oshin Vartanian . . .' *See:* Vartanian, Oshin et al. 'Architectural design and the brain: Effects of ceiling height and perceived enclosure on beauty judgments and approach-avoidance decisions', *Journal of Environmental Psychology* 41, March 2015, pp. 10–18.

## Chapter 5: Status objects versus personal objects

Page 70: 'Talya B. Rechavi, of New York's City University . . .' *See:* Rechavi, Talya B. 'A room for living: Private and public aspects in the experience of the living room', *Journal of Environmental Psychology* 29 (1), March 2009, pp. 133–43.

Page 73: 'This is why Michael Gamble . . .' *See:* Post, Rachel. 'Are tiny houses and micro-apartments the future of urban homes?', *Guardian*, Monday 25 August 2014.

## Chapter 6: Space sharing

Page 75: 'The effect of how many people . . .' *See:* Baum, Andrew, John R. Aiello and Lisa E. Calesnick. 'Crowding and personal control: social density and the development of learned helplessness, *Journal of Personality and Social Psychology* 36, 1978, pp. 1000–1011.

Page 76: 'A study in the *Journal of Personality and Social Psychology* . . .' *See:* Desor, Janet A. 'Toward a psychological theory of crowding', *Journal of Personality and Social Psychology* 21 (1), 1972, p. 79.

Page 77: 'In an ingenious study conducted by the psychologist Leonard Bickman . . .' *See:* Bickman, Leonard et al. 'Dormitory Density and Helping Behavior', *Environment and Behaviour* 5 (4), 1973, pp. 465–90.

Page 77: Desor, Janet A. 'Toward a psychological theory of crowding.' *Journal of Personality and Social Psychology* 21.1 (1972): 79.

## Chapter 7: The stamp of personality

Page 82: 'The main aim of research by the social psychologist Sam Gosling . . .' *See:* Gosling S.D., S.J. Ko, T. Mannarelli and M.E. Morris. 'A room with a cue: personality judgments based on offices and bedrooms', *Journal of Personality and Social Psychology* 82(3), March 2002, pp. 379–98.

Page 83: 'A study by Nils Myszkowski . . .' *See:* Myszkowski, Nils and Martin Storme. 'How personality traits predict design-driven consumer choices', *Europe's Journal of Psychology* 8 (4), 2012.

Page 87: 'Associate Professor Carl Matthews . . .' *See:* Matthews, Carl, Caroline Hill, F. Duncan Case and Tom Allisma. 'Personal bias: the influence of personality profile on residential design decisions', *Housing and Society* 37 (1), 2010.

Page 90: 'The influential American psychologist George Kelly . . .' *See:* Kelly G. *The Psychology of Personal Constructs,* Norton, New York, NY, 1955.

### Chapter 8: Tailor-made homes

Page 93: 'According to Mike Hardwick . . .' *See:* http://www.self-build.co.uk/why-self-build

Page 100: 'Perhaps it is time to heed the words . . .' *See:* Gordon, Elizabeth. *House Beautiful,* April 1953. The editorial was written in response to ongoing institutional promotion of the International Style, which she deplored as 'barren' and promoting unlivable homes. She specifically condemned the architects Walter Gropius, Ludwig Mies van der Rohe and Le Corbusier.

### Chapter 9: Street life

Page 107: 'The eminent psychologist Christopher Alexander . . .' A theory presented in his highly influential book *A Pattern Language: Towns, Buildings, Construction*, Center for Environmental Structure Series, 17 August 1978.

Page 111: 'More recently, Dr Suzanne Hall . . .' *See:* Hall, Suzanne M. 'Super diverse street: A 'transethnography' across migrant localities', *Ethnic and Racial Studies* 38(1), 2015, pp. 22–37.

Page 114: 'In his book *The Blank Slate* . . .' *See:* Pinker, Steven. *The Blank Slate: The Modern Denial of Human Nature*, Viking-Penguin, New York, 2002, pp. 10–11.

Page 116: 'Hieronymus C. Borst and colleagues . . .' *See:* Borst, Hieronymus C., Henk M.E. Miedema, Sanne I. de Vries, Jamie

M.A. Graham, Jef E.F. van Dongen. 'Relationships between street characteristics and perceived attractiveness for walking reported by elderly people', *Journal of Environmental Psychology* 28 (4), December 2008, pp. 353–361.

Page 117: 'In a study conducted by Sarah Foster . . .' *See:* Thesis (Ph. D.) – University of Western Australia, 2010: http://repository.uwa. edu.au:80/R/?func=dbin-jump-full&object_id=29971 &silo_library=GEN01

Page 117: 'Jonathan Gallimore . . .' *See:* Gallimore, J.M., B.B. Brown and C.M. Werner. 'Walking routes to school in new urban and suburban neighborhoods: An environmental walkability analysis of blocks and routes', *Journal of Environmental Psychology* 31(2), 2011, pp. 184–191.

Page 118: 'An interesting study . . .' *See:* Fitzpatrick, Cole D. 'The effect of roadside elements on driver behavior and run-off-the-road crash severity', master's thesis, February 2014: http://scholarworks.umass.edu/theses/1037.

Page 118: 'Kazunori Hanyu . . . ' *See:* Hanyu, Kazunori. 'Visual properties and affective appraisal in daylight', *Journal of Environmental Psychology* 20 (3), September 2000, pp. 273–84.

Page 119: 'Further evidence for this is provided by Masatake Ikemi . . .' *See:* Ikemi, Masatake. 'The effects of mystery on preference for residential façades', *Journal of Environmental Psychology* 25 (2), June 2005, pp. 167–73.

Page 119: 'According to Yui Motoyama . . .' *See:* Motoyama, Yui and Kazunori Hanyu. 'Does public art enrich landscapes? The effect of public art on visual properties and affective appraisals of landscapes', *Journal of Environmental Psychology* 40, December 2014, pp. 14–25.

Page 120: 'Donald Appleyard . . .' *See:* Appleyard, D. 'The environmental quality of city streets: The residents viewpoint', *Journal of the American Planning Association* 35, 1969, pp. 84–101.

Page 120: '(These findings were replicated . . .' The article is based on work undertaken for a Master's dissertation by Joshua Hart MSc while studying at the Centre for Transport and Society at the University of the West of England (UWE). To download the full dissertation, follow the link from Hart, J., Parkhurst,

G., (2011) on the following webpage: http://www.transport. uwe.ac.uk/publications/publications.asp

Page 121: 'This RANCH project . . .' *See:* Matherson, M.I. et al. 'Noise and health. The effects of road traffic and aircraft noise exposure on children's episodic memory: the RANCH project', 12 (49), October–December 2010, pp. 244–54.

Page 121: 'The combination of noise . . .' *See:* Jeon, Jin Yong, Pyoung Jik Lee and Jin You. 'Perceptual assessment of quality of urban soundscapes with combined noise sources and water sounds', *Journal of Acoustical Society of America* 127 (3), 2010, pp. 1357– 66.

Page 122: 'Neil Weinstein . . .' *See:* Weinstein, Neil D. 'Community noise problems: Evidence against adaptation', *Journal of Environmental Psychology* 2 (2), June 1982, pp. 87–97.

Page 124: 'Evy Öhrström . . .' *See:* Öhrström, Evy, Emina Hadzibajramovic, Maria Holmes and Helena Svensson. 'Effects of road traffic noise on sleep: Studies on children and adults', *Journal of Environmental Psychology* 26 (2), June 2006, pp. 116– 126.

Page 125: 'Research conducted in northern India . . .' *See:* Shankar, S., C. Stevenson, K. Pandey, S. Tewari, N.P. Hopkins and S.D. Reicher. 'A calming cacophony: Social identity can shape the experience of loud noise', *Journal of Environmental Psychology* (36), December 2013, pp. 87–95.

Page 127: 'Jasmin Honold . . .' *See:* Honold, Jasmin, Reinhard Beyer, Tobia Lakes and Elke van der Meer. 'Multiple environmental burdens and neighborhood-related health of city residents', *Journal of Environmental Psychology* 32 (4), December 2012, pp. 305–317.

Page 131: 'Visiting behavior was compared . . .' *See:* Carp, Frances. 'Environmental effects upon the mobility of older people', *Environment and Behaviour* 12 (2), 1980, pp. 139–56.

Chapter 10: Protecting the territory

Page 134: 'In New York state . . .' *See:* Rubenstein, H., T. Motoyama and P. Hartjens. 'Defensible space – crime prevention through urban design and architectural design for crime prevention (a methodological review), *The Link Between Crime and the Built*

*Environment* 2, American Institutes for Research: Center for Effective Collaboration and Practice, USA, 1980.

Page 140: 'Building on the results of the New York study . . .' *See:* Brown, Barbara B., and Irwin Altman. 'Territoriality, defensible space and residential burglary: An environmental analysis', *Journal of Environmental Psychology* 3.3, 1983, pp. 203–220.

## Chapter 11: The spirit of place

Page 143: 'Defining a sense of place . . .' *See:* Gustafson, Per. 'Meaning of place: everyday experience and theoretical conceptualizations', *Journal of Environmental Psychology* 21 (1), March 2001, pp. 5–16.

Page 153: 'In an attempt to explore the importance of history . . .' *See:* Lewicka, Maria. 'Place attachment, place identity, and place memory: Restoring the forgotten city past', *Journal of Environmental Psychology* 28 (3), September 2008, pp. 209–31.

Page 153: 'Related to Lewicka's research . . .' *See:* Wells, Jeremy C. and Elizabeth D. Baldwin. 'Historic preservation, significance, and age value: A comparative phenomenology of historic Charleston and the nearby new-urbanist community of L'On', *Journal of Environmental Psychology* 32 (4), December 2012, pp. 384–400.

Page 154: 'Dr Hernan Casakin . . .' *See:* Casakin, Hernan and Miriam Billig. 'Effect of settlement size and religiosity on sense of place in communal settlements', *Environment and Behaviour* 41 (6), 2009, pp. 821–835.

Page 155: 'For example, people who lived in Radom . . .' *See:* Halicz, K. *'Stopień identyfikacji z miejscem w mieście satelickim na przykładzie Radomia'* ('Place attachment in the satellite town: The case of Radom'), unpublished research, University of Warsaw, 2003.

Page 157: The Omnibus profile of Eric Lyons, 'The More We Are Together' is part of the BBC4 Architecture Collection, first broadcast in 1969 and available on iplayer in the UK.

## Chapter 12: Vertigo and other fears

Page 164: 'According to the environmental psychologist Robert Gifford . . .' *See:* Gifford, Robert. 'The consequences of living in high-rise buildings' *Architectural Science Review* 50 (1), 2007, pp. 2–17.

Page 164: 'In New York City, when suicide rates . . .' *See:* Marzuk, P.M., A.C. Leon, K. Tardiff, E.B. Morgan, M. Stajic and J.J. Mann. 'The effect of access to lethal methods of injury on suicide rates', *Archives of General Psychiatry* 49, 1992, pp. 451–58.

Page 165: 'A study in Singapore . . .' *See:* Lester, David. 'Suicide by jumping in Singapore as a function of high-rise apartment availability', *Perceptual and Motor Skills* 79 (1), 1994, pp. 74–74.

Page 166: 'A standout study from the 1980s . . .' *See:* Saegert, S. 'A systematic approach to high density settings: Social and physical environmental factors' in M. R. Gurkaynak and W. A. LeCompte, *Human Consequences of Crowding,* New York: Plenum Press, 1979, pp. 67–82.

Page 166: 'Such disenfranchisement is likely to be reflected . . .' *See:* Franck, K. 'Community by design', *Sociological Inquiry* 53, 1983, pp. 289–311.

Page 166: 'In a nationwide survey . . .' *See:* 'Public priorities in urban Canada: A survey of community concerns', Canada Mortgage and Housing Commission, Ottawa: CMHC, 1979.

Page 166: 'In a study of fresher students . . .' *See:* Holahan, C.J. and B.L. Wilcox. (1979). 'Environmental satisfaction in high-rise and low-rise residential settings: A Lewinian perspective' in J. R. Aiello & A. Baum (eds), *Residential Crowding and Design,* New York: Plenum Press, 1979, pp.127–140.

Page 171: 'The psychologist Christopher Bagley . . .' *See:* Bagley, C. 'The built environment as an influence on personality and social behavior: A spatial study' in D. Canter & T. Lee (eds), *Psychology and the Built Environment,* London: Wiley, 1974, pp. 156–62.

Page 172: 'A study of 558 families . . .' *See:* Fanning, D. M. 'Families in flats', *British Medical Journal* 4, 1967, pp. 382–86.

Page 172: 'As alluded to in the introduction . . .' *See:* Bagley, C. op. cit.

Page 176: 'One study of Elahieh . . .' *See:* Aminzadeh, B. 'High rise impacts on urban environment case study: Alahieh-Tehran', *Journal of Environmental Studies*, March 2001, pp. 105–116.

## Chapter 13: Making better high-rises

Page 180: 'Increasing complexity in this way . . .' *See:*

- Hagerhall, Caroline M., Terry Purcell and Richard Taylor. 'Fractal dimension of landscape silhouette outlines as a predictor of landscape preference', *Journal of Environmental Psychology* 24 (2), 2004, pp. 247–55.
- Moshaver, Mehrdad Karimi and Hamidreza Abrar Asari. 'The effect of tall facades complexity on the aesthetic quality of urban landscape (The case study: Tehran-Iran)', *Applied Mathematics in Engineering, Management and Technology* 2 (5), 2014, pp. 146–56.

Page 184: 'Individuals living in well-designed middle-income high-rise blocks . . .' *See:* Mackintosh, E. 'High in the city', *EDRA: Environmental Design Research Association* 13, 1982, pp. 424–34.

## Chapter 14: Child's play

Page 187: 'In his book *Last Child in the Woods* . . .' *See:* Louv, Richard. *Last Child in the Woods: Saving our children from nature-deficit disorder*, Algonquin Books, 2008.

Page 188: 'Dr Magdalena Czalczynska-Podolska . . .' *See:* Czalczynska-Podolska, Magdalena. 'The impact of playground spatial features on children's play and activity forms: an evaluation of contemporary playgrounds' play and social value', *Journal of Environmental Psychology* 38, 2014, pp. 132–42.

Page 190: 'One study documented . . .' *See:* Huttenmoser, M. 'Children and their living surroundings', *Children's Environments* 12, 1995, pp. 403–13.

## Chapter 15: Adults are kids, too: green spaces

Page 196: 'Agnes van den Berg . . .' *See:* Van den Berg, Agnes E., et al. 'Green space as a buffer between stressful life events and health', *Social Science & Medicine* 70 (8), 2010, pp. 1203–10.

Page 197: 'A study in Helsinki . . .' *See:* Tyrväinen, Liisa, Ann Ojala, Kalevi Korpela, Timo Lanki, Yuko Tsunetsugu and Takahide Kagawa. 'The influence of urban green environments on stress relief measures: A field experiment', *Journal of Environmental Psychology* 38, June 2014, pp. 1–9.

Page 197: 'When people who engaged in gardening . . .' *See:* Hawkins, Jemma L. et al. 'Allotment gardening and other leisure activities for stress reduction and healthy aging", *HortTechnology* 21 (5), 2011, pp. 577–85.

Page 197: 'A study in Dundee, Scotland . . .' *See:* Thompson, Catharine Ward, et al. 'More green space is linked to less stress in deprived communities: Evidence from salivary cortisol patterns', *Landscape and Urban Planning* 105 (3), 2012, pp. 221–29.

Page 198: 'Idit Shalev of Ben-Gurion University . . .' *See:* Shalev, Idit. 'Pictorial and mental arid landscape images reduce the motivation to change negative habits', *Journal of Environmental Psychology* 45, 2016, pp. 30–39.

Page 199: 'Research in Sweden . . .' *See:* Van den Berg, Agnes E., op. cit.

Page 200: 'As Burden says . . .' *See:* Burden, Amanda. 'How public spaces make cities work', ted.com, topic Architecture: https://www. ted.com/talks?sort=newest&topics%5B%5D=architecture &q=Burden

Page 208: '. . . a study in Holland . . .' *See:* Völker, Sebastian, and Thomas Kistemann. 'The impact of blue space on human health and well-being–Salutogenetic health effects of inland surface waters: A review', *International Journal of Hygiene and Environmental Health* 214 (6), 2011, pp. 449–60.

Page 206: 'Mathew White and his colleagues . . .' *See:* White, Mathew, et al. 'Blue space: The importance of water for preference, effect, and restorativeness ratings of natural and built scenes', *Journal of Environmental Psychology* 30 (4), 2010, pp. 482–93.

Page 207: 'Returning to the urban setting . . .' *See:* Kweon, Byoung-Suk, et al. 'Anger and stress: the role of landscape posters in an office setting', *Environment and Behavior* 40 (3), 2008, pp. 355–81.

Page 208: 'A group of researchers categorised . . .' *See:* Wheeler, Benedict W., et al. 'Does living by the coast improve health and wellbeing?', *Health & Place* 18 (5), 2012, pp. 1198–1201.

Page 209: 'One research project, using data from the British Household Panel Survey . . . ' *See:* White, Mathew P., et al. 'Coastal proximity, health and well-being: results from a longitudinal panel survey', *Health & Place* 23, 2013, pp. 97–103.

Page 209: 'This seems to be especially true . . .' *See:* Ashbullby, Katherine J., et al. 'The beach as a setting for families' health promotion: A qualitative study with parents and children living in coastal regions in Southwest England', *Health & Place* 23, 2013, pp. 138–47.

Page 210: 'Ellis Woodman . . .' *See:* Woodman, Ellis, Phineas Harper and Manon Mollard. 'Architecture & Water: Part 1 – The river as city and landscape', *Architectural Review*, 21 October 2014.

Page 210: 'The Moroccan architect Aziza Chaouni . . .' *See:* Eng, Karen. 'A jewel of the city: Aziza Chaouni on restoring the Fez River', TEDBlog, 4 April 2104:

http://blog.ted.com/from-an-open-sewer-to-a-jewel-of-the-city-aziza-chaouni-on-uncovering-and-restoring-the-fez-river/

Page 216: 'A systematic review . . .' *See:* Thompson Coon, Jo, et al. 'Does participating in physical activity in outdoor natural environments have a greater effect on physical and mental wellbeing than physical activity indoors? A systematic review', *Environmental Science & Technology*, 45 (5), 2011, pp. 1761–72.

Page 217: 'In a heartwarming study . . .' *See:* Caddick, Nick, Brett Smith and Cassandra Phoenix. 'The effects of surfing and the natural environment on the well-being of combat veterans', *Qualitative Health Research* 25 (1), 2015, pp. 76–86.

**Chapter 16: Recreational buildings**

Page 221: 'Some of the early observational research . . .' *See:* Sommer, Robert. 'Studies in personal space', *Sociometry* 22 (3), 1959, pp. 247–60.

Page 226: 'Dr Michal Dębek . . .' *See:* Dębek, Michał. 'What drives shopping mall attractiveness?', *Polish Journal of Applied Psychology* 13, 2015, pp. 67–118.

Page 227: 'Dr Jukka Pätynen . . .': *See:* Pätynen, Jukka and Tapio Lokki. 'Concert halls with strong and lateral sound increase the emotional impact of orchestra music', *The Journal of the Acoustical Society of America* 139 (3), 2016, pp. 1214–24.

**Part Six: The Workplace**

Page 233: 'Dr Peter Barrett . . .' *See:* Barrett, Peter. 'The impact of classroom design on pupils' learning: Final results of a holistic, multi-level analysis', Academy of Neuroscience for Architecture (ANFA) article, 11 March 2015

**Chapter 17: Open-plan?**

Page 238: 'Jungsoo Kim . . .' *See:* Kim, Jungsoo and Richard de Dear. 'Workspace satisfaction: The privacy–communication trade-off in open-plan offices', *Journal of Environmental Psychology* 36, 2013, pp. 18–26.

Page 240: 'According to the designers Camenzind Evolution . . .' *See:* https://www.dezeen.com/2013/02/15/google-tel-aviv-by-camenzind-evolution/

Page 240: 'Research has shown that over time . . .' *See:* Pejtersen, Jan, et al. 'Indoor climate, psychosocial work environment and symptoms in open-plan offices.' *Indoor Air* 16 (5), 2006, pp. 392–401.

Page 241: 'Alena Maher . . .' *See:* Maher, Alena, and Courtney von Hippel. 'Individual differences in employee reactions to open-plan offices', *Journal of Environmental Psychology* 25 (2), 2005, pp. 219–29.

Page 241: 'Research by the Indoor Environment Laboratory . . .' *See:* Haapakangas, Annu, Valtteri Hongisto, Jukka Hyönä, Joonas Kokko and Jukka Keränen. 'Effects of unattended speech on performance and subjective distraction: The role of acoustic design in open-plan offices', *Applied Acoustics* 86, December 2014, pp. 1–16.

Page 241: '3. A masking background noise' Pink noise was used to block out the noise caused by speech. Pink noise is like white noise except that the volume is the same across the frequency range.

Page 242: 'The participants completed tests . . .' Working memory tests included the N-back task. This involves showing a series of letters to the participant, who must press a button when a target letter is the same as the letter presented one letter back (1-back) or two letters back (2-back).

Page 242: 'Helena Jahncke . . .' *See:* Jahncke, Helena, et al. 'Open-plan office noise: Cognitive performance and restoration', *Journal of Environmental Psychology* 31 (4), 2011, pp. 373–82.

Page 244: 'They contain a pigment called Opn4 . . .' *See:* Foster, Russell G., Mark W. Hankins and Stuart N. Peirson. 'Light, photoreceptors, and circadian clocks', *Circadian Rhythms: Methods and Protocols*, 2007, pp. 3–28.

Page 244: 'Mirjam Münch . . .' *See:* Münch, Mirjam et al. 'Effects of prior light exposure on early evening performance, subjective sleepiness, and hormonal secretion', *Behavioral Neuroscience* 126 (1), 2012, p. 196.

Page 245: 'A study by Breanne K. Hawes . . .' *See:* Hawes, Breanne K. 'The effects of fluorescent versus LED lighting on soldier tasks in military tents', *Proceedings of the Human Factors and Ergonomics Society Annual Meeting* 58 (1), SAGE Publications, 2014.

Page 246: 'Georg Hoffmann . . .' *See:* Hoffmann, Georg, et al. 'Effects of variable lighting intensities and colour temperatures on sulphatoxymelatonin and subjective mood in an experimental office workplace', *Applied Ergonomics* 39 (6), 2008, pp. 719–28.

Page 247: 'Ruth Raanaas . . .' *See:* Raanaas, Ruth K., et al. 'Benefits of indoor plants on attention capacity in an office setting', *Journal of Environmental Psychology* 31 (1), 2011, pp. 99–105.

Page 247: 'Internal recycling increased . . .' *See:* Bakó-Biró, Zs, et al. 'Ventilation rates in schools and pupils' performance', *Building and Environment* 48, 2012, pp. 215–23.

Page 247: 'A study based in a primary school . . .' *See:* Pegas, P. N., et al. 'Could houseplants improve indoor air quality in schools?', *Journal of Toxicology and Environmental Health* Part A 75.22–23, 2012, pp. 1371–80.

Page 248: 'However, an office-based study . . .' *See:* Kwallek, N., et al. 'Impact of three interior color schemes on worker mood and performance relative to individual environmental sensitivity', *Color Research and Application* 22 (2), 1997, pp. 121–32.

Page 249: 'Researchers at Cornell University . . .' *See:* Tom, Steve PhD, P.E. 'Managing energy and comfort: Don't sacrifice comfort when managing energy', *ASHRAE Journal* 50.6, 2008, pp. 18.

## Part Seven: Healing spaces

Page 253: 'In his book *The Architecture of Happiness* . . .' *See:* de, Botton, Alain. *The Architecture of Happiness*, New York: Pantheon, 2006.

## Chapter 19: A healthy atmosphere

Page 257: 'According to architect Anne Underhaug . . .' *See:* https://mosaicscience.com/story/building-healthier-hospitals

Page 258: 'Ulrich's research . . .' *See:* Ulrich, Roger. 'View through a window may influence recovery', *Science* 224.4647, 1984, pp. 224–25.

Page 258: 'Professor Virginia Lohr . . .' *See:* Lohr, Virginia I., and Caroline H. Pearson-Mims. 'Physical discomfort may be reduced in the presence of interior plants', *HortTechnology* 10 (I), 2000, pp. 53–8.

Page 259: 'Researchers at the Faculty of Social and Behavioural Sciences . . .' *See:* Dijkstra, Karin, Marcel E. Pieterse and A. Th H. Pruyn. 'Individual differences in reactions towards color in simulated healthcare environments: The role of stimulus screening ability', *Journal of Environmental Psychology* 28.3, 2008, pp. 268–77.

Page 261: 'The psychologist Lucy Maddox . . .' *See:* https://mosaicscience.com/story/building-healthier-hospitals

Page 265: 'Nurses tended to visit . . .': For a summary of these and similar studies, *see:* Dijkstra, Karin, Marcel Pieterse and Ad Pruyn. 'Physical environmental stimuli that turn healthcare facilities into healing environments through psychologically mediated effects: systematic review', *Journal of Advanced Nursing* 56.2, 2006, pp. 166–81.

Page 265: 'Barbara Crisp . . .' *See:* Crisp, Barbara. *Human Spaces: Life-Enhancing Designs for Healing, Working, and Living,* Rockport Publishers, 1998.

Page 265: 'Elizabeth Marcheschi . . .' See: Marcheschi, Elizabeth, et al. 'The influence of physical environmental qualities on the social climate of supported housing facilities for people with severe mental illness,' *Issues in Mental Health Nursing,* 2013.

## Further Reading

Alexander, Christopher, *A Pattern Language,* Oxford University Press USA, 1980.

Bachelard, *The Poetics of Space,* Beacon Press, 1992.

Jacobs, Jane, *The Death and Life of Great American Cities,* Pimlico New Ed edition, 2000.

Loos, Adolf, *Ornament and Crime,* Ariadne Press, 1998.

Tsui, Eugene, *Evolutionary Architecture: Nature as a basis for design,* John Wiley & Sons, 1999.

# Index

# Image Credits

Alamy (VIEW Pictures Ltd / Alamy Stock Photo) 23, 25, 171, 193, (Chicago History Museum / Contributor) 32 *left*, (YAY Media AS / Alamy Stock Photo) 32 *right*, (robertharding / Alamy Stock Photo) 38 *right*, (Marco Secchi / Alamy Stock Photo) 41 *top*, (Ian G Dagnall / Alamy Stock Photo) 41 *bottom*, (Arcaid Images / Alamy Stock Photo) 100, 273, (Iain Masterton / Alamy Stock Photo) 117, (Geoffrey Taunton / Alamy Stock Photo) 149, (Arco Images GmbH / Alamy Stock Photo) 150, (Chris Mattison / Alamy Stock Photo) 172, (Megapress / Alamy Stock Photo) 182, (TravelCollection / Alamy Stock Photo) 217, (LusoArchitecture / Alamy Stock Photo) 232 *top*, (imageBROKER / Alamy Stock Photo) 232 *bottom*, (Ian Shipley ARC / Alamy Stock Photo) 250; Getty (Lee Balterman / Contributor) 13, (ullstein bild / Contributor) 39, (Chicago History Museum / Contributor) 32 *left*, (View Pictures / Contributor) 132, 139, (BEN STANSALL / Staff) 177, (GIUSEPPE CACACE / Staff) 184; Michael Moran / OTTO, 153; Paileen Currie, 205; Paul Keedwell, 38 *left*; Ronald C. James, 46; Willem Diepraam, 255.

# Acknowledgements

Thank you to my tutors at the The Sir John Cass School of Art, Architecture and Design for planting the seeds of this book, Lucy Maddox for her advice on hospital design, Dame Maggie Hattersley, my ever encouraging agent and friend and Lucy Warburton of Aurum Press for her patient editing when deadlines slide.